Immersed
in the Lord & Lovin' It

Ian Wilkinson

WestBow
P R E S S
A DIVISION OF THOMAS NELSON

Unless otherwise identified, Scriptures quotations are
from the New King James Version copyright 1982 Thomas
Nelson Inc. Used by permission. All rights reserved.

Scripture quotations marked NLT are taken from the Holy
Bible New Living Translation copyright 1996 Tyndale House
Publishers. Used by permission. All rights reserved.

WestBow Press books may be ordered through booksellers or by contacting:

WestBow Press
A Division of Thomas Nelson
1663 Liberty Drive
Bloomington, IN 47403
www.westbowpress.com
1-(866) 928-1240

Because of the dynamic nature of the Internet, any web addresses or
links contained in this book may have changed since publication and
may no longer be valid. The views expressed in this work are solely those
of the author and do not necessarily reflect the views of the publisher,
and the publisher hereby disclaims any responsibility for them.

Any people depicted in stock imagery provided by Thinkstock are models,
and such images are being used for illustrative purposes only.

Certain stock imagery © Thinkstock.

ISBN: 978-1-4908-0062-2 (sc)
ISBN: 978-1-4908-0061-5 (hc)
ISBN: 978-1-4908-0063-9 (e)

Library of Congress Control Number: 2013912007

Printed in the United States of America.

WestBow Press rev. date: 11/18/2013

Preface

I am a teacher in the body of Christ that focusses on foundations. God has gifted me to impart understanding of the simple truths of the Word in order to equip saints to do the work of the ministry. As you read this book please take my definitions of biblical words and use them in your personal Bible reading and it should bring clarity to your understanding of the Word.

Immersed is my third book on the kingdom of God. I've designed it to be an easy read. My purpose in writing it is to get believers thinking that the lordship of Jesus is actually a good thing. Confessing Jesus as Lord in order to be saved actually translates to the concept of living under his lordship for the rest of your life. I want to convey that living under his lordship empowered by His grace is the best life possible.

God is looking for those that will become the Word manifested in the flesh. He wants the Word to be incarnate (made alive) in us. He wants us to become like Jesus. In short, God desires that we grow up to be the sons of God mentioned in Romans 8:14–19. The word "son" in the Greek language is *huios* (wee-ohs) and means a mature son who reflects the image of his father. Jesus said, "If you've seen me you've seen the Father." Jesus is the Huios of God.

Romans 8:14 tells us that the huios of God are those who are led by the Spirit. Our goal should be to mature to the point we are governed by the Spirit and become the Word incarnate. All of creation is eagerly waiting for the huios of God to be revealed.

Huios can heal the sick and raise the dead. They operate with kingdom authority. They can bring Heaven's resources to earth. They are bondservants of the Lord. They are the ones that have immersed themselves totally in the lordship of Jesus and are lovin' it.

Ian Wilkinson

Acknowledgements

I want to thank the following for their teaching and contributions to my understanding: evangelist John Lucas pastor of Immanuel Church in Calgary back in the 70's, prophet Keith Hazell, James Thomas dean of faculty Pentecostal seminaries in the Ukraine, Bible Temple Portland, Canadian Bible teacher Ern Baxter, English Bible scholar Derek Prince, apostle Bob Terrill from Texas, Kenneth and Gloria Copeland teachers and prophets in the Faith movement, David Pawson Bible teacher in Guildford, England, Randy Clark of Global Awakening, and Bill Johnson of Bethel Church, Redding to name a few of the ones that have contributed to my Christian growth through their books, teaching and leadership.

I would also like to thank the saints at the New Life Centre Canmore and at Huios House for their support and input over the 30 years I have been here in Canmore.

I want to thank my scuba diving buddy - my daughter, Jaana - for posing for the front cover. I should mention my other children Jason and Kristen also scuba dive. And I want to thank my wife, Melodie for allowing me to spend hours at the computer, writing. She doesn't dive but she does walk the beach a lot.

Ian Wilkinson

Table of Contents

Chapter 1: Immersed in the Love of God

> "That Christ may dwell in your hearts through faith; that you, being rooted and grounded in love, may be able to comprehend with all the saints what is the width and length and depth and height - to know the love of Christ which passes knowledge; that you may be filled with all the fullness of God." Eph. 3:17–19

The love of God has <u>four</u> dimensions. Normally we just consider three - height, width and length. It wasn't until I learned to scuba dive that I experienced four dimensions. When diving, one needs to know where they are in relation to the surface (depth), in relation to the bottom (height), forward and backward motion (length) and side to side motion (width). There are four dimensions to God's love because we are totally **immersed** in it. That is something to think about.

This book is about being rooted and grounded in God's love and in his Word. God is love. The Word is God. So we are looking at being rooted and grounded in God. This book is about being totally immersed in God. In order to scuba dive one must learn the basics. Is it the same in the kingdom of God?

Is there a need today for knowing the basics? Absolutely! We need to know kingdom basics if we are to plumb the depths of the Word of God. We need to hear and understand what Jesus said, if we are to be successful.

"Therefore hear the parable of the sower: When anyone hears the message of the kingdom, and does not understand it, then the wicked one comes and snatches away what was sown in his heart." Matt. 13:18–19

"But he who received seed on the good ground is he who hears the word and <u>understands</u> it, who indeed bears fruit and produces: some a hundredfold, some sixty, some thirty." Matt. 13:23

The key to spiritual success is in understanding the message of the kingdom. "And He said to them, "Do you not understand this parable? How then will you understand all the parables?" (Mark 4:13)

To be successful - to be filled with all the fullness of God - starts with knowing the love of Christ. It starts with understanding the basics. Have you been immersed in the basics of the kingdom of God?

A Musing 1: The King James Bible

My first Bible, a King James Version, was given to me by my grandmother over 50 years ago. One of the nice things about reading the King James Version is the opportunity to learn a foreign language. I read in the KJV that Jesus could not enter a town because of the "press". I immediately understood that the paparazzi were a big problem 2000 years ago.

Some versions of the Bible try to capture the intent of the phrases (overall meaning) whereas other versions try to be accurate in the word for word translation. The first type is great for reading but many prefer the second for study. The New Living Translation is a great reading Bible. The New King James is a great study Bible.

My favourite verse from the old KJV is James 1:2 "Count it all joy when you fall into diver's temptations." I love scuba diving and I count it a joy when tempted to go diving. I usually go scuba diving when we are in Maui on vacation. My wife does not dive. I don't think she even goes into the ocean. So I usually take a course every winter just to have someone to dive with. I am two courses away from being a master diver. I love being immersed in the crystal clear waters of the Pacific Ocean and I hope one day to dive the Red Sea.

Diving is a lot of fun but some people are afraid to go diving. I explain to them that it is easier than swimming because if you sink you can still breathe. Breathing is very important when scuba diving. You have a limited amount of air and you want to have relaxed breathing. You can be more relaxed if you trust your equipment. This equipment allows you to enter another world. You have been equipped by God with the Holy Spirit. You can trust him to take you deeper into his world.

Chapter 2: The Love of God

God's love for us contains elements of affection but it is primarily about his commitment to us. God does not have commitment issues. He is committed to those he created and especially to those he is in covenant with. The Greek word used in the New Testament for God's love is *agape*. It is pronounced ag-a-pay. Agape means a commitment to do right regardless of emotion.

Sometimes I want to write "irregardless" but that means "without no regard", which is a confusing double negative, whereas regardless means "without regard". God's love for us is not affected by mood swings. It is steady. It is constant.

One of the most useful Bible studies we have done was to find verses that speak of God's love for us and his ongoing commitment to be for us and with us. As a church we collated over a hundred verses that confirm his love (commitment) for us. Here are some sample quotations.

Gen. 28:15   "Behold, I am with you and will keep you wherever you go,"

Deut. 31:23   "Then He inaugurated Joshua the son of Nun, and said, 'Be strong and of good courage; for you shall bring the children of Israel into the land of which I swore to them, and I will be with you.'"

2 Chron. 16:9   "The eyes of the Lord search the whole earth in order to strengthen those whose hearts are fully committed to him."

Mal. 1:2   "I have loved you (deeply)," says the Lord."

Isaiah 41:10   "Fear not, for I am with you; be not dismayed, for I am your God. I will strengthen you, Yes, I will help you. I will uphold you with my righteous right hand.'"

Matt. 1:23 "Look! The virgin will conceive a child! She will give birth to a son, and they will call him Immanuel, which means 'God is with us.'"

Rom. 1:7 "I am writing to all of you in Rome who are loved by God and are called to be his own holy people." (NLT)

Rom. 5:5 "And this hope will not lead to disappointment. For we know how dearly God loves us, because he has given us the Holy Spirit to fill our hearts with his love." (NLT)

Rom. 8:31–32 "What then shall we say to these things? If God is for us, who can be against us? He who did not spare His own Son, but delivered Him up for us all, how shall He not with Him also freely give us all things?" (NLT)

God is with us and God is for us.

Many Christians keep a journal, which is a great idea. Why not consider collating your own list of verses that confirm God's commitment towards you? You don't have to start a huge Bible study. Simply record verses you come across in your daily Bible reading in a section of your journal. Record any verses that say God is with us, God is for us or God loves us. In a couple months you will have fifty or more verses. It will greatly affirm his love for you.

A Musing 2: God's Word is Alive!

The Word of God is alive. "For the Word of God is living and powerful, and sharper than any two-edged sword, piercing even to the division of soul and spirit and is a discerner of the thoughts and intents of the heart." (Heb. 4:12) It is alive to the extent that it can actually discern the thoughts of our hearts. I can't even always discern the intents of my own heart, yet the Word of God can. Sometimes we forget that the scriptures are alive. We sometimes think that the Word is the letter of the law. Religion and tradition kill the living Word and make it into the letter of the law.

My passion is to become led or governed by the Spirit. I don't like to use the word passion but zeal is no longer in fashion. My heartfelt desire is to learn to walk in the Spirit - to hear and obey the Holy Spirit. Could that be your desire as well? I don't want to just be governed by the Spirit I want to exercise the power of the Spirit. That's what I'm all about - equipping the saints to do the work of the ministry by learning to know and obey the voice of God for themselves.

God speaks today. Those of us who are well acquainted with the gifts of the Spirit - like prophecy and words of knowledge, know God speaks today. I have heard God's voice in my head. I am glad when God speaks to me. Still, the greatest message from God that still speaks today is the Bible.

"Today if you will hear his voice" is repeated three times in Hebrews 3 and 4. It is referring to hearing what God is saying in his Word. It is not referring to the prophetic word but the written word. In Greek "word" is *logos*. Hebrews 4:12 says the logos is alive and powerful. If we are to become led of the Spirit and do the works of Christ then we must allow the Word of Christ to dwell in us richly. It is interesting to see Colossians 3:16 and

Ephesians 5:18 together. As you read them notice the similarities. The Word and the Spirit work together.

"Let the word of Christ dwell in you richly in all wisdom, teaching and admonishing one another in psalms and hymns and spiritual songs, singing with grace in your hearts to the Lord. And whatever you do in word or deed, do all in the name of the Lord Jesus, giving thanks to God the Father through Him." Col. 3:16–17

"And do not be drunk with wine, in which is dissipation; but be filled with the Spirit, speaking to one another in psalms and hymns and spiritual songs, singing and making melody in your heart to the Lord, giving thanks always for all things to God the Father in the name of our Lord Jesus Christ," Eph. 5:18–20

The way we learn to know God's voice is to read the Scripture. Jesus returned from the wilderness, after being tempted by the adversary, empowered by the Spirit. He defeated the adversary with the Word. If we desire to be powerful in the Spirit it helps to have God's powerful and living Word abide in our heart. So read the Word, and it doesn't have to be the King James Version, even though I suspect that the KJV was the version the Apostle Paul used. I'm just kidding.

Chapter 3: Agape

The word "love" in English has diverse meanings and connotations. You can love ice cream, which means you enjoy eating it. You can love TV, which means you enjoy watching it. You can be "in love", which can connote romantic attraction, or in some cases, lust. You can love your child. In that case, love could mean strong affection, attachment or commitment. You can love the past which might mean sentimental feelings. Love has many meanings. And the lack of a precise meaning can lead to confusion when you seek to comprehend God's love.

The basic meaning of agape or God's kind of love is commitment to do right. That does not mean the absence of affection, but it is best for the time being, to focus on the major element of his love - commitment. He is committed to do right for us regardless of emotion. We are to love him with agape also. Our love is a commitment to do right, or in other words, to obey.

"For this is the love of God, that we keep His commandments." 1 John 5:3

When I say "regardless of emotions" I am not suggesting that God is a Vulcan like Mr. Spock. I am not saying God has no emotions. I am saying that if God is angry or if he is joyful, it doesn't affect the quality or quantity of his love for us. As far as we are concerned, he is always in a good frame of mind. His commitment is consistent. It started at creation.

When Adam and Eve sinned they were cast out of the garden and cut off from the tree of life. They were not cut off from God's love. Nothing can separate us from God's love. He is committed to us.

"For God so loved the world that He gave His only begotten Son, that whoever believes in Him should not perish but have everlasting life. For God did not send His Son into the world to condemn the world, but that the world through Him might be saved." John 3:16–17

"Who shall separate us from the love of Christ? Shall tribulation, or distress, or persecution, or famine, or nakedness, or peril, or sword? As it is written: 'For Your sake we are killed all day long; we are accounted as sheep for the slaughter.' Yet in all these things we are more than conquerors through Him who loved us. For I am persuaded that neither death nor life, nor angels nor principalities nor powers, nor things present nor things to come, nor height nor depth, nor any other created thing, shall be able to separate us from the love of God which is in Christ Jesus our Lord." Rom. 8:35–39

God is committed to us. It is a basic truth upon which we can build understanding.

When I was in teacher training at the University of Calgary, I had to do a couple rounds of student teaching. I had to prepare lessons and teach high school students under the supervision of a cooperating teacher. One day my university appointed supervisor came to the school to observe and evaluate how I was doing. Some of my fellow student teachers worried about these evaluations. I wasn't worried.

I entered the Faculty of Education as a "degree after" student. I already had a Bachelor of Science degree. I was a bit older than the kids who went into Education straight from High School. Some of the kids were terrified of their supervisors. They felt that they really needed to impress them. So they prepared special lessons with large amounts of dazzle for the day the supervisor would be present. One of my fellow student teachers went as far as to con her class into responding with enthusiasm to each of her questions.

On the other hand, I knew something about how things worked. The University is in many ways a business like any other, and the faculty of Education's purpose is to produce teachers. Somehow I knew that my supervisor was not out to fail me but to insure my success. I taught a normal lesson and asked him for his advice on what I could have done better. He was happy.

We need to see the Lord as someone committed to our success. He is not out to fail us but to insure we succeed.

Agape is a commitment to do right. What is right? That's a good question, but before addressing it let's examine the concept a bit. You know that fruit of the Spirit is love (a commitment to do right) joy, peace, and so on.

"But the fruit of the Spirit is love, joy, peace, longsuffering, kindness, goodness, faithfulness, gentleness, self-control. Against such there is no law. And those who are Christ's have crucified the flesh with its passions and desires. If we live in the Spirit, let us also walk in the Spirit." Gal. 5:22–25

Hopefully you are also aware that the kingdom of God is righteousness, peace and joy in the Holy Spirit. "For the kingdom of God is not eating and drinking, but righteousness and peace and joy in the Holy Spirit. For he who **serves** Christ in these things is acceptable to God and approved by men." (Rom. 14:17–18)

Righteousness in this passage means doing right. So connect the two thoughts and we see that the fruit of the Spirit is a commitment to do right and the kingdom of God includes "doing right". The concepts are practically the same. Doing what is right, in context with agape, is to do what God wants done - to do the will of God. He tells us what he wants us to do principally through his Word. That is why the love of God in 1 John 5:3 is to do his commands. He wants us to do his will. "Not everyone who says to me, 'Lord, Lord,' shall enter the kingdom of heaven, but he who does the will of my Father in heaven. Many will say to me in that day, 'Lord, Lord, have we not prophesied in Your name, cast out demons in Your name, and done many wonders in Your name?' And then I will declare to them, 'I never knew you; depart from me, you who practice lawlessness!'" Matt. 7:21–23

In recent past, very few in the church were in danger of saying to the Lord "We prophesied in your name, cast out demons and have done many wonders in your name." Very few were operating in the supernatural. This warning is a bit more pertinent today as we start to see many moving out in healing and miracles. Prophecy and words of knowledge are becoming less rare.

Randy Clark of Global Awakening has activated many of the saints (born-again believers in Christ) into words of knowledge, healing and miracles. He directs those he teaches to minister first in the love of God before ministering in the supernatural. In that way, if the person being ministered to doesn't get healed, he won't interpret it as God rejecting him. This method of instruction allows the saints to develop in the supernatural but still stay grounded. Randy Clark also emphasizes the need to be consistent in personal prayer and Bible reading because what we **are** is more important than what we **do**. We want what we do to reflect what we are.

Since the love of God is a commitment to do what is right in God's eyes, we want to attempt as best we can to keep to the written word of God. Jesus had a highly developed sense of doing right. He only did what he saw the Father doing. He only spoke what he heard the Father speaking. That is where I would like to be. Is that where you would like to be? It will require that we learn to walk in the Spirit. (Gal. 5:25) Getting to that place requires that we know and practice the basics.

The Matthew 7 passage shows that Jesus isn't after lip service. If you say he is Lord, then you'd better do what he says. You can also see that it is possible to use supernatural gifts without being properly connected to the Lord. Our goal is to know Jesus, not just do the supernatural. We want to do the works of Jesus in the will of the Father. We want to be partnered with him not acting independent of him.

Is it possible to get carried away with the supernatural and lose focus? Matthew 7 says it is. Jesus told them, "I never knew you; depart from me." Honestly if someone was to come to your church and do prophecy, deliverance and miracles you'd be happy and amazed. I know I would. I would assume that he had his act together and walked in faith. I would be so impressed with the miracles that I would assume that what he believed and taught was true.

Simon the sorcerer tried to purchase miracle power. He wasn't properly aligned with the Lord. There is a possibility that one could do miracles and yet practice lawlessness. Practising lawlessness means that what they did was not authorized or initiated by the Lord. Love - is a commitment to do what is righteous – to do what is authorized. Let's move in the supernatural while at the same time maintain focus. If we are governed or led of the Spirit, what we do will be authorized.

Love is a commitment to do what God authorizes.

A Musing 3: Seek First the Kingdom of God

Years ago I pastored a church in Canmore. The previous pastor had taught for two years on the grace of God. I read in John's gospel that Jesus was full of grace and truth so I decided to spend some time teaching about truth. What I discovered was that many times when Jesus said, "I tell you the truth" the next thing he said was about the kingdom of God. So my research on the subject of truth pointed me to the kingdom of God.

I decided to take Matthew 6:33 seriously, and began to seek the kingdom diligently. I discovered as I looked into the subject of the kingdom, that I really knew little about it. I was, in fact, king dumb. I learned that the kingdom of God is the central topic of the Gospels, and yet I knew very little about it. Books I read seemed to assume the reader knew what it was. No one bothered to define it. Then about six months into my seeking for the meaning of the kingdom, I found a little book by Ern Baxter that explained it. He defined the kingdom of God as the government of God.

As I began to teach the church about the kingdom, I discovered that they also knew little of the kingdom. They too were king dumb. Then as I spoke to different congregations in the States and the UK, I found out most of the saints were not really clear about the meaning of the kingdom. I call this the kingdom paradox - the people called to preach the kingdom don't know what it is exactly.

It's hard to seek something if you don't really know what it is you are supposed to seek.

It's hard to preach the kingdom if you are king dumb.

Chapter 4: The Kingdom of God

> "For the kingdom of God is not eating and drinking, but righteousness and peace and joy in the Holy Spirit. For he who serves Christ in these things is acceptable to God and approved by men." Rom. 14:17–18

Jesus actually spoke quite a bit about the kingdom of God. Matthew's Gospel uses the term "kingdom of heaven", but it means the "kingdom of God". Eighty percent of the parables are about the kingdom of God. We are to preach the gospel of the kingdom. The Sermon on the Mount and the Lord's Prayer both reference the kingdom. In fact the kingdom is the central theme of the gospels. After his resurrection, Jesus continued to talk about his kingdom.

"The former account I made, O Theophilus, of all that Jesus began both to do and teach, until the day in which He was taken up, after He through the Holy Spirit had given commandments to the apostles whom He had chosen, to whom He also presented Himself alive after His suffering by many infallible proofs, being seen by them during forty days and speaking of the things pertaining to the kingdom of God." Acts 1:1–3

Paul also spoke about the kingdom. It must be very important. "Then Paul dwelt two whole years in his own rented house, and received all who came to him, preaching the kingdom of God and teaching the things which concern the Lord Jesus Christ with all confidence, no one forbidding him." (Acts 28:30–31)

Sometimes Biblical words can become religious jargon. Such is the case with kingdom. Let's strip "kingdom" of its religious layers and get to the core meaning. A kingdom is a form of government. It is a monarchy or rule of one. In the kingdom of God there is one ruler. You confess his name in order to be saved. "That if you confess with your mouth the **Lord** Jesus and believe in your heart that God has raised Him from the dead, you will be saved. For with the heart one believes unto righteousness, and with the mouth confession is made unto salvation." (Rom. 10:9–10)

The kingdom of God is the government of God or the rule of Christ. So when you read Matt. 6:33, it is saying to make it a priority to be ruled by Christ. Rom. 14:18 tells us the kingdom is about serving Christ. When you see the phrase "kingdom of God" it is about being governed by the Spirit of God as opposed to being controlled by sin. No one wants more government. We aren't talking about **more** government. We are talking about replacing bad government with good government.

A Musing 4: The Sinner's Prayer

> "That if you confess with your mouth the Lord Jesus and believe in your heart that God has raised Him from the dead, you will be saved. For with the heart one believes unto righteousness, and with the mouth confession is made unto salvation." Rom. 10:9–10

In many churches today the Biblical concept of confessing that Jesus is Lord has been replaced with the Sinner's Prayer. It is an invitation asking the Saviour to enter my heart. Although the Sinner's Prayer has served to introduce people to Jesus, it is in many ways inadequate and misleading.

The confession which brings salvation is a confession of heart faith in the Lord. To believe in your heart that God raised Jesus from the dead can be explained by an earlier mention in Romans that Jesus was <u>declared to be God</u> by being raised from the dead. "Lord" is the name of God, so essentially you must believe that Jesus is God and call on his name, "Lord", to be saved. The Sinner's Prayer doesn't really emphasize that Jesus is Lord. Yet that is the vital component if confession is to be made unto salvation.

"For with the heart one believes". What is the heart? What does the Bible mean by "heart"? The organ in your chest, which we call the heart, is a blood pump. It is a muscle. It is not the seat of affections or emotions. It is a muscle that pumps blood. The word "heart" in the Bible means inner core. References to heart include: that it is the source of speech, that it is a place of thinking, and that it contains a storehouse of memories. Faith of the heart is a deep abiding faith - one that is totally convinced. It is like the faith you have in a chair that you have sat in countless time. You know it will hold your weight because it has held it thousands of times.

In the Sinner's Prayer you ask Jesus into your heart. You "receive" Jesus in your heart. That is a confusing concept, since Jesus is a man. It would be like having a very large tumour. The Bible expressly teaches to <u>believe</u> in the Lord and to <u>receive</u> the Spirit. He is not a tumour. The believing and receiving are two distinct steps in the four steps of the new birth.

Calling on the Lord has an implied dynamic that having done that, you are prepared to continue with your life with the new paradigm, in which you have an owner and master.

A Musing 5: Kingdom Theology

To muse means to think. Amuse means not to think. I prefer things that are both amusing and thought provoking. Is that an oxymoron or a paradox? These musings are random thoughts similar to rabbit trails. Sometimes rabbit trails are most interesting.

My wife, Melodie, and I went to Sao Paulo, Brazil with Global Awakening. There were about eighty of us in the group that went. Pat Bock was the director in charge of us. He would put notices at everyone's hotel room door, informing us when we could exchange money. He wanted to be covert about it. Instead of using the official name for Brazilian currency, the "Real", he called it "rabbit" exchange. Sometimes finding him and his real money was a trial. You could say a rabbit trial. Pat is the international director of Global Awakening but he lets Randy Clark do the pulpit ministry. Pat is an avid reader – reading up to one or two pages a day. He is currently reading my last book, and I hope it's not a trial for him.

Kingdom theology is a wonderful thing to understand. Since the kingdom of God is the central theme of the Gospels and in my humble opinion the whole Bible, it almost seems too obvious to note that knowing kingdom theology can be very useful.

Kingdom theology is different from church based theology - which is the theology most of us have absorbed through osmosis over the years. Kingdom theology centres on the **Lord** Jesus. All other truth is understood within the context of his Lordship. Church based theology is salvation based theology. It's sometimes called "me-centred" theology. It focusses on the **Saviour** and how He caters to us. In church based theology Bible teachings are understood within a framework of salvation.

For example, in kingdom theology, obedience to God is considered the proper response to our Lord and master. In salvation based theology, obedience to God is seen as a vain attempt to be justified by works. In kingdom theology tithing is seen as paying the Lord, the portion that belongs to him as a way of honouring his lordship and ownership of the earth. In church centred theology it is seen as a fund raising device designed to pay church staff salaries. These few examples show us some of the differences between church based and kingdom based thinking. Jesus instructed his followers to preach the gospel of the kingdom.

Knowing kingdom theology allows one to evaluate any new teaching he hears. Having a framework of good kingdom theology also provides a filing system for remembering teachings. We are not to be blown about by every wind of doctrine. It is good to be anchored with kingdom-based theology. What is kingdom-based theology? It is primarily a way of looking at the Bible from the perspective that Jesus is first and foremost, Lord.

Chapter 5: Born Again

In the context of the kingdom or government of God, "born again" means to come under new management. We are to come under the rule of Christ.

"And having been set free from sin, you became slaves of righteousness...For when you were slaves of sin, you were free in regard to righteousness. What fruit did you have then in the things of which you are now ashamed? For the end of those things is death. But now having been set free from sin, and having become slaves of God, you have your fruit to holiness, and the end, everlasting life. For the wages of sin is death, but the gift of God is eternal life in Christ Jesus our Lord." Rom. 6:18, 20–23

As a born-again Christian, I am free of sin's control. I have come under new government - good government. I am no longer a slave of sin, but a slave of righteousness. Righteousness means doing right. Love is a commitment to do right. I am now to walk under love's influence.

The Bible calls giving in to sin's passions and allowing it to control us - walking in the flesh. Walking in the flesh is bad. Your human body is not bad but giving in to sin's control is bad - very bad. We are susceptible to leaning in this direction, which is why we need God's government. We are to seek his kingdom first.

"Therefore do not worry, saying, 'What shall we eat?' or 'What shall we drink?' or 'What shall we wear?' For after all these things the Gentiles seek. For your heavenly Father knows that you need all these things. But seek first the kingdom of God and His righteousness, and all these things shall be added to you. Therefore do not worry about tomorrow, for tomorrow will worry about its own things. Sufficient for the day is its own trouble." Matt. 6:31–34

When you are a slave of sin, you have limited resources. When you are a slave of God, you have unlimited resources. You can see by the context which Matthew 6:33 sits in, that God is prepared to meet all your needs. You can trust him. You need not worry. "My God shall supply all your needs according to his riches in glory." (Phil 4:19) Not only does he know your needs, he wants to supply them. One must only come under new management. One must seek first the rule of Christ. It is a priority.

Seeking to be ruled by Christ is a daily decision. Jesus taught us to pray this way.

"Our Father in heaven, hallowed be your name. Your kingdom come. Your will be done on earth as it is in heaven. Give us this day our daily bread. And forgive us our debts, as we forgive our debtors. And do not lead us into temptation, but deliver us from the evil one. For yours is the kingdom and the power and the glory forever. Amen." Matt. 6:9–13

God's command to seek his kingdom as a priority shows that it is his will to insure that all believers learn to be led or governed by the Spirit. God wants us to be Spirit-led and walk in the Spirit rather than walk according to the flesh. Seeking the kingdom means a daily volitional surrender to God's rule. "Your kingdom (governing) come; your will be done." There can be no mistake God is saying he wants us to embrace his government. And when we do, we enter into peace and provision. So don't worry! God knows your needs.

The government or rule of Christ is righteousness, peace and joy in the Holy Spirit. The kingdom is in the Holy Spirit. The name of the Holy Spirit is Christ. He is Christ in you. The Christ in you is not Jesus. Jesus is a man. The Christ in you is the Holy Spirit. When we let the Holy Spirit rule we enter into true liberty from sin's control.

In the New Testament, "Christ" can either mean the anointed one (Messiah, Jesus) or the anointing (Spirit) depending on context. When it speaks of the anointing it speaks of the Holy Spirit. Since the kingdom is in the Holy Spirit, it stands to reason that one of the steps in entering the Kingdom is to connect with the Spirit.

You first connect with the Spirit when he convicts you of sin and persuades you that Jesus is Lord. The Spirit assists you in confessing with your mouth that Jesus is Lord. "And no one can say that Jesus is Lord except by the Holy Spirit." (1 Cor. 12:3) Then you connect in a deeper way when you are baptised and filled with the Spirit. Finally you connect in an even deeper way when you learn to hear and obey the Spirit. The kingdom (government) of God is in the Holy Spirit.

The New Birth

The new birth is a four step process. Step one is to repent or change your thinking. Step two is to believe that Jesus is Lord. Step three is to be baptised (immersed) in water. Step four is to be baptised (filled) with the Holy Spirit. The steps don't have to be in this order but all four are important. None should be left out.

The new birth is like natural birth. The baby turns its head towards the birth canal. It comes out of the darkness of the womb into the light of day (or hospital room). Then the umbilical cord is severed and the baby breathes. Or the baby breathes and then the umbilical cord is cut. All four are required in a natural birth. If the baby fails to breath the birth is not successful. If its head does not turn it causes complications such as a breech. If the umbilical cord is not cut it will become infected and death may occur.

The turning of the baby's head is similar to repentance. The birth into light coincides with a decision to believe in the Lord Jesus. The act of cutting of the old support system (the cord connecting baby to mommy) is like water baptism, which cuts us off from sin's control. And the word "breath" in Greek also means spirit. Water baptism and severing the umbilical cord take place once. Being filled with the Spirit and breathing are ongoing practices. The new birth is a process. It is the process of coming under new management.

A Musing 6: The Jesus People

As a child, I attended an Anglican church with my parents. Our church was across the street from the high school. Later when I attended high school I started to go to the Anglican youth group. Anglicans are open-minded so you can find a variety of beliefs in an Anglican church. One year our adult sponsors where a young couple that believed in the Jesus of the Bible. They started having Bible studies in their home. This planted a seed of an idea.

After high school I developed a cancer in my neck and while in hospital I read the Gospel of Matthew with some interest. Sometimes the fear of dying can motivate one to look for God. It wasn't until a year later however, that I heard the gospel message of salvation. A friend from work took me to a Jesus Party sponsored by the Jesus People. The Jesus People had been welcomed by a small Pentecostal Church.

I was born again in the early 70's at that Pentecostal church. There was a major revival. I became part of a move of God in that church. We saw over a thousand people water baptised in a few years. There were over 200 young people attending the church. Many of us were totally immersed in the things of God. We were committed. Our only real interests in life were God and sharing the gospel. In the early years we spent 40 hours per week in church or church related activities. We heard countless guest speakers teaching a variety of doctrines, so we learned to weigh different points of view. We spent hours per week praying and evangelizing. There is something about being born in revival fire that leaves an indelible mark on your life. Nothing else satisfies.

I am thankful for the opportunities that I grew up with in the Jesus People. I was able to lead worship until I became proficient. I was allowed to teach adult Sunday school, which developed my teaching skills. I led the weekly youth meeting for a time, and also led the Thursday and Saturday street evangelism. I was given ample opportunity to preach. I was also house leader in one of the church's residences for kids who were saved off the streets. I was allowed to be active, and not just warm a pew. Many of us shared that experience and ended up in full time ministry. We were sold out totally for God. In my opinion that is the only way to be.

One night a speaker was in the baptismal tank doing baptisms, and he was electrocuted when his microphone shorted out. I guess you could say he was "zaptized". He died. The people prayed and after a while he came back to life. Baptism is supposed to be symbolic of your death and resurrection. This speaker was an awesome teacher. He demonstrated the concept for us. I don't recommend you try this at home.

A Musing 7: The Power of the Blood

The blood of Jesus saves us from sin. I have heard people plead the blood like it is a protective talisman or something. When the children of Israel were told to put blood on the lintels and doorframes of their houses, it did protect them from the death angel. Egyptians, who followed the same instructions, were also protected from the Angel of Death.

A person who is properly saved is already covered by the blood and does not need to "plead the blood" to be protected. It is not the "pleading" per se, that does the protecting. The protection exists in the reality of our relationship with the Lord Jesus. However, one might find it useful to plead the blood when one is being accused by the devil.

As in a court of law, where one can plead the Fifth Amendment so as not to incriminate oneself, one can face the enemy's accusations in much the same way. Simply admit to the fact if you have sinned and then plead the blood. Because you are covered by the blood, no accusation can get a guilty verdict. Confess, "I may have sinned by doing such and such but as a blood bought saint I am not a sinner. My sins are under the blood." Don't allow the enemy's accusation to stick. Submit to God and resist the devil.

If you are on the street and a gun battle breaks out, standing up and pleading the Fifth will not stop a bullet. Angels on the other hand can stop bullets. God's feathers can stop bullets. You might want to consider all the ways God can protect us.

The blood of Jesus has purchased us or redeemed us from sin. We are bought with a price - the blood of Jesus. "For he who is called in the Lord while a slave, is the Lord's freedman. Likewise, he who is called while free, is Christ's slave. You were bought at a price; do not become slaves of men." (1 Cor. 7:22–23)

"Knowing that you were not redeemed with corruptible things, like silver or gold, from your aimless conduct received by tradition from your fathers, but with the precious blood of Christ, as of a lamb without blemish and without spot."1 Peter 1:18–19

The only people who are bought are slaves. Sin used to own us but we have been bought back from sin (redeemed) by the Lord who purchased our redemption with his own blood. This makes us slaves of Christ. "But now having been set free from sin, and having become slaves of God, you have your fruit to holiness, and the end, everlasting life." (Rom. 6:22) The power of the blood is that we are now owned by God.

Chapter 6: Born of Water

"There was a man of the Pharisees named Nicodemus, a ruler of the Jews. This man came to Jesus by night and said to Him, 'Rabbi, we know that You are a teacher come from God; for no one can do these signs that You do unless God is with him.' Jesus answered and said to him, 'Most assuredly, I say to you, unless one is born again, he cannot **see** the kingdom of God.' Nicodemus said to Him, 'How can a man be born when he is old? Can he enter a second time into his mother's womb and be born?' Jesus answered, 'Most assuredly, I say to you, unless one is born of water and the Spirit, he cannot **enter** the kingdom of God. That which is born of the flesh is flesh, and that which is born of the Spirit is spirit. Do not marvel that I said to you, "You must be born again." The wind blows where it wishes, and you hear the sound of it, but cannot tell where it comes from and where it goes. So is everyone who is born of the Spirit.'" John 3:1–8

Read the passage above again looking for the word "saved". It is conspicuously absent. Jesus is not talking about being saved per se, he is talking about seeing and entering the kingdom of God. Now let us insert the basic definition of the kingdom into the verses.

> Unless one is born again he cannot **see**
> the government of God.

> Unless one is born of water and the Spirit
> he cannot **enter** the government of God.

There are four steps in the process of seeing and entering the kingdom. They are the four steps of the new birth. The first two steps involve <u>seeing</u> the government of God. Jesus is king of the kingdom. The first two steps have to do with him. Step one is to change your perception of who Jesus is. You used to think of him as a religious leader, a prophet or perhaps even just a swear word. Your thinking comes into alignment with truth. This change in thinking is called repentance. If you were trying to earn salvation through religious effort, or if you were trying to merit God's love by your good behaviour, that would be called repentance from dead works.

Step two also involves perception. It is a realization of who Jesus is. He is Lord. Seeing Jesus as Lord is the essence of kingdom. You confess that Jesus is Lord and you are saved. "For whoever calls on the name of the Lord shall be saved." (Rom. 10:13) Saved from what? Good question. "Saved" means a lot more than safe from Hell. You confess with your mouth that Jesus is Lord and you believe in your heart that he is God. Technically at this point you **see** the kingdom. Demons also believe in the Lord and tremble. We must go further. We must take steps of obedience that confirm that we perceive Jesus to be our Lord and are prepared to continue in life on that basis. We are not just to give lip service. When we take this step we are planning on doing what the Lord tells us to do. If we actually believe he is Lord then we will live in obedience to him.

Steps one and two let us see the kingdom. There are also two steps in the process of entering his government. Steps three and four of the new birth enable us to enter it.

Step three is to be born of water. Some people think that may refer to a woman's water breaking prior to giving birth. The Greek language did not use "born of water" to describe this and the Hebrew culture likewise used no such idiom. The expression "born of water" did, however, refer to the rite of cleansing used by the Essenes and for the ceremonial cleansing (dipping in water) before entering the Temple. "Born of water" means **immersed** in water (baptism).

"Or do you not know that as many of us as were baptized into Christ Jesus were baptized into His death? Therefore we were buried with Him through baptism into death, that just as Christ was raised from the dead by the glory of the Father, even so we also should walk in newness of life. For if we have been united together in the likeness of His death, certainly we also shall be in the likeness of His resurrection, knowing this, that our old man was crucified with Him, that the body of sin might be done away with, that we should no longer be slaves of sin." Rom. 6:3-6

"For he who has died has been freed from sin. Now if we died with Christ, we believe that we shall also live with Him, knowing that Christ, having been raised from the dead, dies no more. Death no longer has dominion over Him. For the death that He died, He died to sin once for all; but the life that He lives, He lives to God. Likewise you also, reckon yourselves to be dead indeed to sin, but alive to God in Christ Jesus our Lord." Rom. 6:7–11

Nothing represents the transfer from one system of government to the other better than water baptism. Water baptism is like circumcision. It is the cutting of the umbilical cord. It is the cutting off of the flesh. Sin cannot control a dead person. We are buried with Christ. We are cut off from sin's control.

Water baptism means immersion in water (buried in water). It was foreshadowed by the deliverance of the children of Israel from Egypt when they crossed the Red Sea. "Moreover, brethren, I do not want you to be unaware that all our fathers were under the cloud, all passed through the sea, all were baptized into Moses in the cloud and in the sea," (1 Cor. 10:1–2)

The children of Israel were baptized into Moses (in the cloud and in the sea). We are baptized into Christ in the Spirit (cloud) and in water. There are two baptisms - water and Spirit. Hebrews 6:2

mentions these doctrines of baptisms. Water baptism saves us. (1 Pet. 3:20–21) Saves us from what? Good question!

"In the days of Noah, while the ark was being prepared, in which a few, that is, eight souls, were saved through water. There is also an antitype which now saves us - baptism (not the removal of the filth of the flesh, but the answer of a good conscience toward God), through the resurrection of Jesus Christ," 1 Pet. 3:20-21

From what did the baptism in the Red Sea save the children of Israel? The complete army of Egypt was destroyed. The power of Egypt to control them was destroyed. The power of sin to control you is destroyed in water baptism. You can still choose to sin but sin can't make you do it.

Baptism means to immerse. We are immersed in the water that separates us from the old life. This is a great word picture of your new life in God. Serving God is not a little add-on to your life. It is something you become totally **immersed** in. We are immersed in God's love and immersed in water.

Immersion in water is a vital step in discipleship. The steps of discipleship should parallel the steps of the new birth should they not? We would want those we disciple to experience all the steps in the new birth. We are to make disciples, which includes preaching the kingdom and then baptizing them.

"And Jesus came and spoke to them, saying, 'All authority has been given to me in heaven and on earth. Go therefore and make disciples of all the nations, baptizing (immersing) them in the name of the Father and of the Son and of the Holy Spirit, teaching them to observe all things that I have commanded you; and lo, I am with you always, even to the end of the age.' Amen." Matt. 28:18–20

This passage is called the great commission. In the past forty years of church life it might be called the great omission. We no longer seem to make disciples, we make converts. But let's look closely at what Jesus said.

"All authority has been given to me in Heaven and in earth" means nothing less than Jesus is Lord. He is pointing out who he is. "Go therefore" means go because your Lord tells you to go. "Make disciples" means make apprentices. "Of all the nations" means from all people groups. Apprenticing is an experience based teaching method not a lecture based teaching style.

"Baptizing them (immersing them) in the name of the Father, the Son and the Holy Spirit," means we use proper names. Father is not a name. The name of the Father was given to Moses as part of his commission to save the children of Israel. Moses was told that the forever name of God was Yahweh or Lord.

"Moreover God said to Moses, "Thus you shall say to the children of Israel: 'The Lord, God of your fathers, the God of Abraham, the God of Isaac, and the God of Jacob, has sent me to you. This is my name forever, and this is my memorial to all generations.'" Ex. 3:15

"And God spoke to Moses and said to him: "I am the Lord. I appeared to Abraham, to Isaac, and to Jacob, as God Almighty, but by my name Lord I was not known to them." Ex. 6:2–3

Father is not a name. The name of the Father is Lord. Lord means owner/master. A lord is, by definition, someone you obey.

Son is not a name. The name of the Son is Jesus. Jesus means saviour. Spirit is not a name. The name of the Spirit is Christ. Christ means anointing or anointed.

We baptize in the name of the Lord Jesus Christ.

"Therefore let all the house of Israel know assuredly that God has made this Jesus, whom you crucified, both Lord and Christ." Now when they heard this, they were cut to the heart, and said to Peter and the rest of the apostles, "Men and brethren, what shall we do?" Then Peter said to them, "Repent, and let every one of you be baptized in the name of Jesus Christ for the remission of sins; and you shall receive the gift of the Holy Spirit. For the promise is to you and to your children, and to all who are afar off, as many as the Lord our God will call." Acts 2:36–39

"And he said to them, "Into what then were you baptized?" So they said, "Into John's baptism." Then Paul said, "John indeed baptized with a baptism of repentance, saying to the people that they should believe on Him who would come after him, that is, on Christ Jesus." When they heard this, they were baptized in the name of the Lord Jesus." Act 19:3–5

The commission continues...

"Teaching them to **observe** all that I commanded," could mean that the teaching method that works best is role modelling. New disciples see us obeying and follow our example. "And lo I am with you always," means God's presence goes with us. How does his presence go with us? His Spirit dwells within. God is for us and with us.

"If you love me, keep my commandments. And I will pray the Father, and He will give you another Helper, that He may abide with you forever - the Spirit of truth, whom the world cannot receive, because it neither sees Him nor knows Him; but you know Him, for He dwells with you and will be in you. I will not leave you orphans; I will come to you." John 14:15–18

The disciples were told to wait until the Holy Spirit was imparted to them. (See Acts 1:4) Then on the Day of Pentecost they were baptised in the Holy Spirit.

So far the great commission has these elements:

1) Jesus is Lord (steps 1 and 2 - seeing the kingdom)

2) Make skilled followers by immersing them (step 3 - entering the kingdom)

3) Teach them to obey my commands which included the command to be filled with the Spirit (step 4 - entering the kingdom)

A close look at the great commission reveals that the four steps of the new birth are repeated in the plan to make disciples. We are to make disciples, which includes insuring they are properly born-again with all four steps of the new birth.

A Musing 8: Frank and Gene

Back in the 70's with the Jesus People after most services we had a baptismal service. Following that we had a wrap-up service of praise and worship. We would sing and dance and celebrate Jesus. One night we went fairly late and Frank, one of the leaders of a Jesus People group home, had to get up early the next day. Sometime after midnight the worship leader asked for song requests. Frank suggested, "Thou hast Turned My Mourning into Dancing for Thee".

One night there were people at the front worshipping. Suddenly there was a large CRACK sound. Gene had gone down - slain in the Spirit. He hit the front edge of a pew with the back of his head which made this terrific crack sound. Back in those days we hadn't received the memo about catching people. If they were slain, they went down on their own. Mind you we didn't push anyone down either. We did, however, have the little modesty blankets. They were useful.

Later I asked Gene how it felt to hit his head. He said that it felt as if he had fallen on pillows. Maybe it's a good thing to get smacked upside of the head once in a while. We could call it Gene therapy. We'll let God administer this therapy though. Recently my wife was slain in the Spirit and no one caught her. She ended up with a large lump on the back of her head, so perhaps I should retract my comment about it being a good thing to be smacked upside the head.

A Musing 9: Dunking Donuts

Baptism means to immerse. The Greek word *"baptizo"* was anglicised to baptism. Baptism took on a religious meaning. Baptizo means to dip. Policemen in Greece baptize their donuts in coffee. Back in the day when the KJV was written, the church in England sprinkled. They didn't dip. So the translators at the time thought it prudent to simply Anglicize baptizo into "baptism" rather than translate it as "dip". Can you visualize a Greek policeman baptizing his donut?

It is funny how some words lose their simple meanings and get a religious connotation that fits with the traditions of men. Those traditions make the Word of none effect. It's almost as if a malevolent being or force was at work trying to corrupt our understanding of the Word of God. I write a column for a Calgary based newspaper called City Light News. The column is called "Seeing in High Definition." It is about defining biblical words that have been muddied through time by tradition. Baptism is a clear example.

Immersion in water is the first step of obedience taken by a new believer. It is a step of faith. It is the obedience of faith. Without faith it is ineffective. Immersion in water, in the name of Jesus is a physical act with spiritual consequences. Without faith it is only a physical act that gets you soaking wet.

I taught a DTS for YWAM in the Ukraine. DTS means Disciple-ship Training School. YWAM means youth without any money. I taught a group of 25 to 30 young eager disciples the four basic steps of coming under new management: repentance, faith, water baptism and Spirit baptism. Some of them had not yet been dipped, so we dipped them, and some had not yet being filled with the Holy Spirit, so we prayed for them and they were filled. At the end of my week the director thanked me for having the courage to tackle such controversial topics. I was a bit shocked she would say that. I didn't realize the simple basics were controversial but I guess in some places they are. The simple truths can become complicated. It's almost as if a malevolent being or force was at work trying to corrupt our understanding of the Word of God.

I was christened as a baby, but when I decided to follow Christ I was baptized in His name because I was committed to follow Christ - to do what is right. That is not a decision someone else can make for you, is it?

Why not take a minute? You deserve a coffee break. Are you craving a donut? Dunk a donut or grab a cookie that you can baptize in hot chocolate.

Chapter 7: Born of the Spirit

The fourth step in seeing and entering the government of God is to be baptized in the Spirit. This is not to be a single event but an ongoing experience. It parallels breathing. When a baby is born and the umbilical cord is severed, it must breathe in order to get oxygen. It goes from one life support system to another. The baby must be fed milk, since the food energy from mother's blood no longer is exchanged through the umbilical cord. A spiritual baby needs to breath the Spirit and must feed on the milk of the Word.

We looked at John 3:1–8 where Jesus shared about seeing and entering the kingdom of God. We noted at the time that salvation was not the theme. Most Evangelicals would equate being born again with being saved, but we see from scripture that a more accurate meaning of born again would be "to come under new management". In the process of coming under new management or becoming a disciple we are properly and excellently saved. Jesus did not commission the church to get people saved per se. He commissioned us to make disciples.

All one has to do to be saved, is call on the name of the Lord. The thief on the cross that confessed that Jesus is Lord was saved. He was not a disciple. He was not baptised unless you consider that he was crucified with Christ. Paul links being crucified with Christ with water baptism - "knowing this, that our old man was crucified with Him, that the body of sin might be done away with, that we should no longer be slaves of sin." (Rom. 6:6) Essentially one can be saved simply by calling on the name of the Lord. So if a victim of a car accident is bleeding out on the side of the road and he prays, "Save me Lord Jesus!" he can expect either to be saved from death or saved from Hell if he dies.

However to function properly in the government of God one must take all four steps:

1) Repent from dead works
2) Believe that Jesus is Lord
3) Be immersed in water in the name of the Lord Jesus Christ
4) Be filled or immersed in the Holy Spirit.

You see these four basics recorded in Acts 8.

"Therefore those who were scattered went everywhere preaching the word. Then Philip went down to the city of Samaria and preached Christ to them. And the multitudes with one accord heeded the things spoken by Philip, hearing and seeing the miracles which he did. For unclean spirits, crying with a loud voice, came out of many who were possessed; and many who were paralysed and lame were healed. And there was great joy in that city." Acts 8:4–8

Philip, a deacon, went to Samaria and preached the government of God to them and did many signs and wonders (deliverances and healings). Many were converted to Christ and were immersed in water. "When they believed Philip as he preached the things concerning the kingdom (government) of God and the name of Jesus Christ, both men and women were baptized (immersed)." (Acts 8:12) The apostles heard that Samaria had received the word of God and Peter and John were dispatched to Samaria.

"Now when the apostles who were at Jerusalem heard that Samaria had received the word of God, they sent Peter and John to them, who, when they had come down, prayed for them, that they might receive the Holy Spirit. For as yet He had fallen upon none of them. They had only been baptized in the name of the Lord Jesus. Then they laid hands on them, and they received the Holy Spirit." Acts 8:14–17

The new believers in Samaria had, under the ministry of Philip, experienced both step two and step three. Step two is to believe in the Lord. Step three is to be immersed in water. Chances are most had also repented, with the obvious exception of Simon the Sorcerer. They had not, however, received the Holy Spirit.

To those that believe that the baptism of the Spirit is automatic at the time confession is made unto salvation, I point out that what is recorded in Acts 8 nullifies that theory completely. The Spirit is active, helping one to confess Jesus is Lord (1 Cor. 12:3), but that is not synonymous with the baptism of the Spirit. Baptism in the Holy Spirit is a separate and vital step. This was recognized by the apostles. How did they know that the Spirit had not yet fallen on them? Good question!

"And when Simon saw that through the laying on of the apostles' hands the Holy Spirit was given, he offered them money, saying, 'Give me this power also, that anyone on whom I lay hands may receive the Holy Spirit.'" (Acts 8:18–19) Something visibly happened when hands were laid on people to receive the Spirit. Simon saw! Yes he saw something tangible occur that actually impressed him more than seeing Philip do healings and miracles. Then Peter confronted Simon and told him to repent. The apostles came to Samaria and completed all four steps of seeing and entering the kingdom.

What did Simon see?

Chapter 8: Day of Pentecost

"When the Day of Pentecost had fully come, they were all with one accord in one place. And suddenly there came a sound from heaven, as of a rushing mighty wind, and it filled the whole house where they were sitting. Then there appeared to them divided tongues, as of fire, and one sat upon each of them. And they were all filled with the Holy Spirit and began to speak with other tongues, as the Spirit gave them utterance. And there were dwelling in Jerusalem Jews, devout men, from every nation under heaven. And when this sound occurred, the multitude came together, and were confused, because everyone heard them speak in his own language. Then they were all amazed and marvelled, saying to one another, 'Look, are not all these who speak Galileans? And how is it that we hear, each in our own language in which we were born? Parthians and Medes and Elamites, those dwelling in Mesopotamia, Judea and Cappadocia, Pontus and Asia, Phrygia and Pamphylia, Egypt and the parts of Libya adjoining Cyrene, visitors from Rome, both Jews and proselytes, Cretans and Arabs - we hear them speaking in our own tongues the wonderful works of God.' So they were all amazed and perplexed, saying to one another, 'Whatever could this mean?' Others mocking, said, 'They are full of new wine.'" Acts 2:1–13

On the day of Pentecost something happened that was observable. It was tangible. Amidst what might have appeared to be people reeling under the influence of alcohol, Galileans had somehow developed the amazing ability to declare the wonderful works of God in multiple languages. People were amazed and perplexed. Something was different about the Pentecost experience than what I experienced at Confirmation.

What I experienced at Confirmation wouldn't have perplexed anyone. It was tame in comparison. In fact one could correctly say that nothing actually happened at my Confirmation even though it was my church's version of being filled with the Spirit. I have evangelical friends who claim to have been baptized in the Holy Spirit simply because they prayed the Sinner's Prayer. We dispelled that theory in the last chapter. Peter and John could have allowed the Samaritan church to be the First Baptist Church but instead they laid hands on them and turned them into Spirit-filled Baptists or Pentecostals.

The infilling of the Holy Spirit must be a real and tangible experience because of the fact that the baptism of the Spirit is **essential** in the new covenant. It is also the basis for our confidence. "You were sealed with the Holy Spirit of promise, who is the guarantee of our inheritance until the redemption of the purchased possession, to the praise of His glory." (Eph. 1:13–14)

Peter preached the government of God to some Gentiles. While he was preaching, the Holy Spirit fell on the Gentile believers. How did the Jewish believers know that the new Gentile believers had received the Holy Spirit? They knew because the baptism of the Spirit is tangible, real, observable and often noisy.

"While Peter was still speaking these words, the Holy Spirit fell upon all those who heard the word. And those of the circumcision who believed were astonished, as many as came with Peter, because the gift of the Holy Spirit had been poured out on the Gentiles also. For they heard them speak with tongues and magnify God. Then Peter answered, 'Can anyone forbid water, that these should not be baptized who have received the Holy Spirit just as we have?' And he commanded them to be baptized in the name of the Lord. Then they asked him to stay a few days." Acts 10:44–48

For they heard them speak with tongues. The baptism of the Spirit is not a secret, silent act we accept by faith. The New Testament wasn't written yet. So they didn't have the option of getting people to put faith in the Gospels and Epistles. Nowadays we can point to the words of Jesus in Luke 11.

"If a son asks for bread from any father among you, will he give him a stone? Or if he asks for a fish, will he give him a serpent instead of a fish? Or if he asks for an egg, will he offer him a scorpion? If you then, being evil, know how to give good gifts to your children, how much more will your heavenly Father give the Holy Spirit to those who ask Him!" Luke 11:11–13

I have used this verse to reassure people who didn't speak in tongues, after I've laid hands on to receive the Holy Spirit. Most people do speak in tongues but some do not. If they don't speak in tongues I want to assure them of the Father's love and his faithfulness. And there is other solid biblical evidence of the power and presence of the Holy Spirit other than tongues. One looks at their hunger for God, their desire to worship, and their enthusiasm to witness. Sometimes the power and presence is visible without the tongues.

But I must be honest, although I believe that you do not need to speak in tongues as evidence of the baptism of the Spirit, the people who don't speak in tongues don't seem all that reassured by Luke 11:13. They would prefer to experience something. I can only assume that there is some kind of blockage - religious expectation, a residue of Cessationist doctrine, or fear - that prevents the flow of tongues. And while I say that I believe it is possible to be filled with the Spirit and not speak in tongues, a survey of the book of Acts will reveal that in every case they did.

So, is my position a concession to experience? Does my doctrine have to adapt to experience or should it be based on the scripture? As a Spirit-filled Baptist, I would say we should stick to the purity of the Word, but as someone who has pastored, I will have to say some things remain a mystery. Even so, the pattern of Scripture is that the baptism of the Spirit is a tangible and audible experience.

A Musing 10: Singing in Tongues

I mentioned that though the pattern of Scripture indicates the baptism of the Spirit is a tangible and audible experience, sometimes our experience doesn't line up. I suspect that in the cases where people don't speak in tongues there is some kind of blockage. The blockage is on the human end, not on God's end, and it may not be the fault of the person praying to receive the baptism of the Spirit. In fact, it is very unlikely that someone seeking to be filled would sabotage their own experience knowingly. They most likely are not consciously aware of blockage.

Common blockages include the following:

1) past teaching against speaking in tongues that has left residual doubt,
2) waiting for the Spirit to actually physically do the speaking,
3) feelings of unworthiness, and
4) fear of sounding foolish.

My personal experience of the baptism of the Spirit was quite exciting. I answered an altar call at Immanuel Church, the Jesus People church in Calgary. The preacher had asked anyone who wanted the Holy Spirit, to come forward so I did. I was met at the front by Keith Hazell who asked me what I wanted. I said I wanted the Spirit. He told me to lift my hands and he prayed I would be filled. I felt electricity flow down my arms into my chest and I began to speak in tongues - easily and fluently. I was, in effect, "zaptized" in the Spirit. Fortunately I wasn't holding a microphone at the time.

I had the advantage of having an Anglican background that did nothing to negate the experience. I was also in a charged atmosphere of tongue talking Jesus People. Keith was an experienced and anointed man of God. I was very open and hungry for the experience and carried no false expectations.

Some people don't have all these advantages and some carry baggage such as Cessationist heresy. Cessationism is the false belief that all the gifts of the Spirit stopped after the New Testament was written. Some people have feelings of unworthiness. These blockages can be overcome with good teaching. Maybe realizing that tongues is for today and is a gift we are all unworthy to receive, will help remove blockages. Maybe one must renounce false teaching in order to move forward. Maybe one must declare that their unworthiness doesn't disqualify them, but in fact is why they need the Spirit.

Some people have an expectation that God will physically do the speaking, so they wait and say nothing. Then we get into giving them advice and techniques that detract from the beauty of the experience. "You must make sound with air moving over your vocal chords." We prompt them with some syllables we hope will initiate a flow. Sometimes that works. Sometimes it doesn't. We tell them it will seem foolish, it will seem like baby talk and it's alright - not to be embarrassed. It's really important to know that God is not rejecting them. He is not the blockage. There are ways around the blockage. One time we got around the blockage in a curious way.

The brain is divided into two hemispheres called left and right. The left brain apparently is the logical thinking centre. The right hemisphere is more creative. We speak with our left hemisphere but we sing with our right.

We were praying with a friend from England to be filled with the Spirit who had some kind of blockage to speaking in tongues. After futile attempts to coax words out of her, I adopted a new tack. I took up my guitar and began to sing. I asked her to sing along in the Spirit. Soon she was singing in tongues. I just had to get her into her "right" mind.

Tongues are vitally important. Praying in tongues is perfect prayer - totally aligned with the will of God. It will aid us and facilitate us to move forward into our spiritual destiny. The idea that all things work together for good is often quoted out of context. All things do work together for good if we have prayed in the Spirit. Read the passage from Romans 8 and see for yourself this concept in context. You will also see how the topic of praying in tongues leads Paul to mention spiritual destiny.

"Likewise the Spirit also helps in our weaknesses. For we do not know what we should pray for as we ought, but the Spirit Himself makes intercession for us with groanings (prayer in tongues) which cannot be uttered. Now He who searches the hearts knows what the mind of the Spirit is, because He makes intercession for the saints according to the will of God. And we know (how do we know?) that all things work together for good to those who love God, to those who are the called according to His purpose. For whom He foreknew, He also predestined to be conformed to the image of His Son, that He might be the firstborn among many brethren. Moreover whom He predestined, these He also called; whom He called, these He also justified; and whom He justified, these He also glorified." Rom. 8:26-30

We know that all things work together because we have prayed in the Spirit. Prayer in the Spirit not only aligns us with destiny but also imparts faith. Praying in tongues edifies or builds faith. "He who speaks in a tongue edifies himself." (1Cor. 14:4) When I pray in tongues I literally imagine obstacles to success and ministry being removed. "What is the conclusion then? I will pray with the spirit, and I will also pray with the understanding. I will sing with the spirit, and I will also sing with the understanding." (1 Cor. 14:15) Both praying and singing in the Spirit are encouraged.

A Musing 11: The Anointing

> "'And it shall come to pass in the last days, says God, That I will pour out of my Spirit on all flesh; Your sons and your daughters shall prophesy, Your young men shall see visions, Your old men shall dream dreams. And on my menservants and on my maidservants I will pour out my Spirit in those days; And they shall prophesy.'" Acts 2:17–18 (Joel 2:28–32)

The anointing is one of the main components (necessities) for ministry. We want ministers to be upright and honest and we also want them to teach what God is saying, not their own opinions. We want the words they say to be authored by God. God said he would pour out his anointing on sons and daughters, on young and old and on menservants and maidservants. God anoints both genders of all ages for ministry. I have a friend, Harry Sani Alufazema, in Malawi, Africa whom I visit from time to time. I go there to teach about the kingdom to pastors.

Harry once asked me if women could be ministers. What do you think? The word "minister" actually means servant. To minister means to serve. Let me adjust the question. Can women be servants? Yes, of course, they're already servants. Does God anoint woman to serve? Well it says clearly in the passage above that he does. Can we appoint what God anoints? I hope we can and do. Perhaps the question Harry was asking was, "Can woman hold positions of responsibility in the church?"

The Bible teaches that older woman should teach the younger. (Titus 2:3–4) Paul commended Phoebe our sister who is a servant (deacon) of the church. (Rom. 16:1) Priscilla was Paul's fellow worker. (Rom. 16:3)She was a member of an apostolic team. Anna was a prophetess. (Luke 2:36) She was a valid witness with

Simeon that the Saviour was born. Her witness was not rejected because of gender. God anoints both genders.

God has appointed leadership in families. The two "elders" in a family are the father and the mother. In our church most of our elders are couples. "For as many of you as were baptized into Christ have put on Christ. There is neither Jew nor Greek, there is neither slave nor free, there is neither male nor female; for you are all one in Christ Jesus." (Gal. 3:27–28)

The bride of Christ has both men and women. The sons of God (Rom. 8:14) includes both genders. God anoints both menservants and maidservants. William Booth said that some of his best men were women. The real questions are, "Do you want leaders that are anointed by the Lord?" and "How do you recognize true anointing?"

Chapter 9: "Reviewing the Situation"

To be successful - to be filled with all the fullness of God - starts with knowing the love of Christ. It starts with knowing the basics.

God is with us and God is for us.

That God is committed to us and to our success, is a basic truth upon which we can build understanding. We need to see the Lord as someone committed to our success. He is not out to fail us but to insure we succeed.

Agape - the God kind of love - means a commitment to do right regardless of emotion.

The kingdom of God is the central theme of the Gospels. It is very important.

The simple definition of the kingdom of God is the government of God or the rule of Christ.

Read the kingdom parables and substitute "government" for "kingdom". Make it a habit of substituting government of God or rule of Christ in place of kingdom of God throughout the New Testament until your mind is reprogrammed - and the religious jargon is displaced.

We see and enter the kingdom by four steps:

1) Repent from dead works
2) Believe that Jesus is Lord
3) Be immersed in water in the name of the Lord Jesus Christ
4) Be filled or immersed in the Holy Spirit.

In the book of Acts we see that the apostles insured that all four steps were completed. The <u>order</u> the steps are done in is not important. What is important is that all four are completed. The four steps constitute the new birth.

"Born again" in a kingdom context means to come under new management. The steps required in making disciples confirm the four steps in the new birth.

The kingdom of God is in the Holy Spirit. We need to be immersed in the Spirit. The Spirit is a seal and a guarantee. He helps us pray. He is essential. He helps us comprehend God's love for us in a personal way.

"For we know how dearly God loves us, because he has given us the Holy Spirit to fill our hearts with his love." Rom. 5:5 NLT

Chapter 10: Love and Marriage

God loves us dearly. The God kind of love is agape - a commitment to do right for another, regardless of emotion. His love is similar to marriage. Marriage is a commitment. Marriage is a covenant. When we are born again into the kingdom of the Lord Jesus we enter into covenant with him.

I have been married 35 years. There have been good years and there have been tough years. Mostly there have been good years. In the tough times it is not emotion that keeps you together, it is commitment. Romance and affection are wonderful and essential but they can ebb and flow. They should be upheld by the solid rock of commitment.

I know the secret to understanding married women. What is it that women want from their husbands? They want to know that they are the most important thing in their husband's life (second only to their commitment to the Lord). Once, after I shared this gem of wisdom at church a woman approached my wife and expressed how great it must be to have a husband that understands. My wife responded by saying that at least I knew the theory.

Normally to enter into a marriage covenant there are four steps. First, the two people must see each other. The girl turns the guy's head in her direction. Then after some time getting to know one another, a decision is made. A proposal is accepted. Then there is a public ceremony in which vows are shared. This is followed by a private consummation. In the case of arranged marriages two families get together and plan. A decision is made. There is a public ceremony and a private consummation.

The first step is like repentance. It involves a change of perception. Attraction causes one to look closer at the possibilities. The second step is making a decision to marry, which is like coming to faith or deciding for Christ. This is a very important step. The third step - the public ceremony - is like water baptism which is a public declaration of your intent to follow Jesus. The fourth step of consummation is like the infilling of the Spirit. The wedding ceremony occurs once, just like water baptism. The act of consummation is ongoing in the life of the couple, just like we need to be filled with the Spirit on an ongoing basis.

"And do not be drunk with wine, in which is dissipation; but be filled with the Spirit, speaking to one another in psalms and hymns and spiritual songs, singing and making melody in your heart to the Lord, giving thanks always for all things to God the Father in the name of our Lord Jesus Christ, submitting to one another in the fear of God." Eph. 5:18–21

The phrase "be filled" in the Greek is actually "be being filled" - the ongoing continuous sense. The baptism of the Spirit is the first of many fillings. It is an essential of the new covenant that we be filled continuously with the Holy Spirit.

When you get married you are no longer independent. When I was teaching in Ternopil, Ukraine my social interpreter was a young woman who had aspirations to be an independent married woman. I laughed. I told her it might be difficult to reach both goals simultaneously. Marriage is a partnership. When we enter the kingdom of God, we actually partner with the Lord. We take his yoke. We are yoked together. We work with him using his strength.

In times past, when a marriage took place, a woman went from her father's house to her husband's house. She went from obeying her father to obeying her husband. She experienced a change of government. This is like the new birth into the kingdom. It is a change of government. Nowadays when a couple gets married there is still a change of government but in many cases, it might be the man who comes under new management.

Marriage represents the kind of government present in the kingdom of God. It is a union of love. The kingdom is structured like a family. It is loving form of government. We are the bride of Christ. We come into his house and live under his rules. He loves us dearly. He laid down his life for us and he will freely give us all things pertaining to life and godliness. God's love is commitment. Marriage is commitment. Marriage is covenant. We are in covenant with God. He loves us dearly.

A Musing 11: Yoke is Easy

> "Come to me, all you who labour and are heavy laden, and I will give you rest. Take my yoke upon you and learn from me, for I am gentle and lowly in heart, and you will find rest for your souls. For my yoke is easy and my burden is light." (Matt. 11:28–30)

When we enter God's government we enter into partnership with him. We take his yoke. A yoke is a device used to link or partner two animals together. God is linked to us - he will never leave us or forsake us.

Sometimes we miss the true intent of Jesus' words because we come from a totally different culture than first century agrarian society. Back in the time when Jesus spoke, they used oxen to pull their plows and carts. Also, the KJV of the Bible used farming terms that we are no longer familiar with. Another factor influences our ability to interpret Scripture. We might not know the rules of grammar.

The context of the quote above is rest. The concept of rest is a very important one. God himself rested on the seventh day. I believe what Jesus is alluding to is - resting from trying to serve God in our own strength. It is an invitation to partner with God, or with the grace of God. The old covenant was one based on obeying God's commands with human strength. The new covenant is about obeying God _using his strength_. When we partner with God our job is to trust and his job is to do what needs doing.

"Take my yoke upon you" is an invitation to partner one on one with him. "I am gentle" is an old expression used by farmers. A gentle ox was an older, experienced ox accustomed to pulling the load (plow or cart) and could keep to a straight course. It was "lowly in heart" meaning it was used to submitting to the will of the master and did not rebel. The older gentled ox was used to "disciple" the younger inexperienced ox. So we see here a word picture that includes an invitation to become Christ's disciple.

"My yoke is easy" doesn't really mean what we think it means. "Easy" was an old fashioned farming term. The farmer would custom fit the yoke to the shoulders of the draft animal. He would "easy" it by carving it and padding it to prevent chaffing. It would be well fitted. So "easy" doesn't mean "not difficult". It means padded and well suited.

"My burden is light" is not the absence of responsibility. Nor is it the call to complete leisure. It is an interesting fact that a single horse may pull a 1000 pound load but when yoked, two horses can pull 6000 - 7000 pounds. So if two animals were yoked and only expected to pull 2000 pounds it would seem light. Jesus is saying, "With me helping you, the load will be much lighter".

So looking at some old farming terms, we can get to a clearer idea of what Jesus was really saying. Now to that we add an insight from grammar.

"My yoke is easy." Yoke is the subject. Easy is the object. We have too often read this as "my blah-blah is easy" and really only seen "easy". "Easy" connotes to our minds as "not difficult". We have put the em - **pha´** - sis on the wrong syl - **la´** - ble. Yoke is the subject and that is where the emphasis should be put. A yoke is basically a device made to extract hard work out of draft animals without inflicting damage on the animals. And while compassion was a factor, the main reason the farmer padded the yoke was to insure a steady flow of work from his "organic tractor". People in Jesus' time would have understood that.

The subject provides the context for the statement. So what we may have read as "my way is not difficult" may in fact really mean "my implement for extracting hard work from you is tailor made to extract that work without damaging you". "For we are His workmanship, created in Christ Jesus, for good works, which God prepared beforehand that we should walk in them." (Eph. 2:10) So it becomes apparent that God doesn't want us to live passively, but to actively work in his kingdom. We are to work partnered with him - operating out of rest - using his divine power to do the work.

Chapter 11: The Old and the New

As Christians we have a covenant with God called the new covenant. God has made a few covenants with mankind starting with Adam. The most important Old Testament covenant was the one made with the children of Israel under Moses. It is called the old covenant. The old covenant, or Mosaic Covenant, carried on from the covenant made with Abraham and was the covenant God made with the Jews. That covenant ended. Some people believe it ended in 30 AD when the veil in the Temple was rent in two. Some people believe it ended when the Temple was destroyed in 70 AD. There may have been a forty year overlap between when the new covenant began in 30 AD and the old covenant ended in 70 AD. The passage below was written prior to 70AD. "First covenant" refers to the old.

"For if that first covenant had been faultless, then no place would have been sought for a second. Because finding fault with them, (the people) He says: 'Behold, the days are coming, says the Lord, when I will make a new covenant with the house of Israel and with the house of Judah - not according to the covenant that I made with their fathers in the day when I took them by the hand to lead them out of the land of Egypt; because they did not continue in my covenant, and I disregarded them, says the Lord. For this is the covenant that I will make with the house of Israel after those days, says the Lord: I will put my laws in their mind and write them on their hearts; and I will be their God, and they shall be my people. None of them shall teach his neighbour, and none his brother, saying, "Know the Lord," for all shall know me, from the least of them to the greatest of them. For I will be merciful to their unrighteousness, and their sins and their lawless deeds I will remember no more.' In that He says, 'A new covenant,' **He has made the first obsolete**. Now what is becoming obsolete and growing old is ready to vanish away." Heb. 8:7–13

A careful reading of the Hebrews passage (You may want to read it again) shows the following:

1) There was a problem with the old covenant.

2) The fault was not with God's end but with the people of Israel. They failed to uphold it.

3) God saw a need for a new covenant. (See Ezekiel 36:26)

4) The purpose of the new covenant was that, from the least to the greatest, all would know God for who he truly is - **Lord**. All would know God personally and correctly as Lord.

5) In the new covenant God would place his law not on two tablets of stone but on two tablets of living tissue, the heart and the mind. The problem was not with the law. The law is good. The law is carried forward into the new covenant.

6) The new covenant makes the old obsolete. The old covenant no longer functions.

7) The old (Hebrews was written circa 64AD) was **becoming** obsolete and ready to vanish away. It wasn't completely gone yet, but soon to be gone. I assume it ended when the Temple was destroyed in 70 AD.

Both the passage from Hebrews (which is a quote from Jer. 31:31) and the passage below are prophetic promises to the children of Israel that God would make a new covenant with them that would enable them to obey his laws. The nations (the Gentiles) would know that he is the Lord.

"Therefore say to the house of Israel, Thus says the Lord God: "I do not do this for your sake, O house of Israel, but for my holy name's sake, which you have profaned among the nations wherever you went. And I will sanctify my great name, which has been profaned among the nations, which you have profaned in their midst; and **the nations (Gentiles) shall know that I am the Lord,**" says the Lord God, "when I am hallowed in you before their eyes. For I will take you from among the nations, gather you out of all countries, and bring you into your own land. Then I will sprinkle clean water on you, and you shall be clean; I will cleanse you from all your filthiness and from all your idols. I will give you a new heart and put a new spirit within you; I will take the heart of stone out of your flesh and give you a heart of flesh. **I will put my Spirit within you and cause you to walk in my statutes,** and you will keep my judgments and do them. Then you shall dwell in the land that I gave to your fathers; you shall be my people, and I will be your God." Ezek. 36:22–28

God said that he would empower his people to obey him. What was it God was going to do? He said he will put his Spirit within them. In the new covenant God writes his law in our hearts and minds. The law teaches us his will. What makes the new covenant so different from the old is the indwelling presence and power of the Holy Spirit. That is why it is essential that one is baptized in the Holy Spirit when one enters the kingdom of God.

There are three components to the covenant. The first two are listed in Ezek. 36:28. The third component is from Matt. 28:20

1) "You shall be my people"
2) "I will be your God"
3) "I am with you always."

I will rewrite the three components as follows:

1) I will be your God   [righteousness]
2) You will be my people   [peace]
3) I will be with you always   [joy]

"I will be your God," simply means that Jesus gets to be Lord of your life - your decisions, your finances, your plans etc. He is the master. You obey his instructions with the power he supplies by the Holy Spirit. "You will be my people," means all the blessings of the covenant belong to you, including salvation, health and prosperity. "I will be with you always," means his presence will go with you and will enable you to do all that is necessary for your success in serving him. This final component is vital. We must learn how to operate out of his strength.

"I will be your God" means God is Lord of your life. It speaks of our commitment to covenant. This idea compares with righteousness. Righteousness means doing the will of the Father. Having a Lord means we obey someone other than ourselves. We do the will of God. We obey his commands. This is love for God, that we obey his commands. Righteousness is the first component of the kingdom of God. The kingdom of God is righteousness, peace, and joy.

Moses was given the name of God the Father - Lord. In the new covenant we are given the law or teachings God the Father gave to Moses. They are written in our heart and mind so that we can know the will of the Father. Love is a commitment to do the will of the Father.

"You will be my people" speaks of God's commitment to us. When we align with his government and come into Father's house then his resources become available to us. As his people we have access to all the benefits of the cross. We have access to blessing. This idea compares to the concept of peace. God's kingdom is a government of peace. Jesus is the Prince of Peace. Peace means much more than the absence of war. It contains peace of mind, health, and wealth. Peace is the path to prosperity.

Jesus is the Prince of Peace and his name means Saviour. Our Saviour saves us from sin, sickness, deception, poverty, and death. Our Saviour enables us to align with the will of the Father. Jesus is our Lord and Saviour. Being in covenant with him includes both obeying his will and being blessed.

"I will be with you always" speaks of the Presence of God. Moses once said to God that he didn't want to go further unless God's presence went with him. In fact, when Moses first met God, he asked him "Who am I that I should go to Pharaoh." And God answered, "I will certainly be with you." Bill Johnson refers to this in his teaching on *The Presence*. He says God's answer to Moses' question "who am I" meant that Moses was someone God liked to be with. You are also someone God likes to be with. God is with you and for you.

In the presence of God is fullness of joy. "I will be with you always" speaks of the ongoing presence and anointing of the Holy Spirit who enables us to do what we are called to do. We are not to obey God with human effort but with God's joy. We can't heal the sick, but God can. God's joy is our strength. The Holy Spirit supplies us with grace.

Aspects of covenant relate to the kingdom and the Godhead.

Covenant	Kingdom	Godhead
I will be your God	righteousness	Father/ Lord
You will be my people	peace	Son/ Saviour
I will be with you always	joy	Holy Spirit/ Anointing

A Musing 12: Knowing God

A diamond has many facets but in substance it is one. God also has many facets. A few of his names include: Father, Saviour, Architect, Captain, High Priest, Prince, Counsellor, Almighty, Healer, Deliverer, Ancient of Days, and Lord. The substance that God is made up of is love. God is love. It says twice in the Bible that God is love.

He is also Lord. Lord is not just a facet of his nature. It is the very essence of his nature. It may interest you to know that God is called Lord over 7000 times in the Bible. That is a message in itself. You don't have to be a mathematical genius to know that 7000 is larger than 2. I am not saying that God is not love just because it only says so twice. He is definitely "love". He is definitely Lord as well. That he is Lord is very important for us to understand. God has had difficulty getting this point across.

"Hear, O heavens, and give ear, O earth! For the Lord has spoken: "I have nourished and brought up children, And they have rebelled against me; The ox knows its owner And the donkey its master's crib; But Israel does not know, (their master) My people do not consider." (who I really am) Is. 1:2–3

God was venting his frustration at the fact this own people didn't get it. The ox knew his owner but Israel did not know its owner. The donkey knew it has a master but Israel did not. Adam and Eve rebelled. Now Israel has rebelled. What was God going to do? We see his plan in the second chapter of Isaiah.

"Now it shall come to pass in the latter days that the mountain of the Lord's house shall be established on the top of the mountains, and shall be exalted above the hills; And all nations shall flow to it. Many people shall come and say, 'Come, and let us go up to the mountain of the Lord, to the house of the God of Jacob; He will teach us His ways, and we shall walk in His paths.' For out of Zion shall go forth the law, and the word of the Lord from Jerusalem." Is. 2:2–3

The time of the latter days is the time of Jesus. The mountain here speaks of a kingdom. The Lord's house is his church. The kingdom of God will be lifted up over all other governments. All nations shall flow to it, means all ethnic groups (Gentiles and Jews) will enter the kingdom. People will say, "Come let us go (first) to his mountain (kingdom) and then into the house (church)". "He will teach us his ways" means we will be discipled. We will walk in the paths of righteousness. For out of Zion (city of God or the people of God) shall go forth his law. {The law is a schoolmaster that brings us to Christ.} The law is possibly used as an evangelistic tool like Ray Comfort does or it could mean the law as in the written Word of God. The word of the Lord from Jerusalem could refer to the prophetic word.

Daniel chapter 2:36–45 helps with the interpretation. It tells us when the kingdom will come.

"This is the dream. Now we will tell the interpretation of it before the king. You, O king, are a king of kings. For the God of heaven has given you a kingdom, power, strength, and glory; and wherever the children of men dwell, or the beasts of the field and the birds of the heaven, He has given them into your hand, and has made you ruler over them all—you are this head of gold. But after you shall arise another kingdom inferior to yours; then another, a third kingdom of bronze, which shall rule over all the earth. And the fourth kingdom (Roman) shall be as strong as iron, inasmuch as iron breaks in pieces and shatters everything; and like iron that crushes, that kingdom will break in pieces and crush all the others. Whereas you saw the feet and toes, partly of potter's clay and partly of iron, the kingdom shall be divided; yet the strength of the iron shall be in it, just as you saw the iron mixed with ceramic clay. And as the toes of the feet were partly of iron and partly of clay, so the kingdom shall be partly strong and partly fragile. As you saw iron mixed with ceramic clay, they will mingle with the seed of men; but they will not adhere to one another, just as iron does not mix with clay. <u>And in the days of these kings the God of heaven will set up a kingdom which shall never be destroyed</u>; and the kingdom shall not be left to other people; it shall break in pieces and consume all these kingdoms, and it shall stand forever. Inasmuch as you saw that the stone was cut out of the mountain without hands, and that it broke in pieces the iron, the bronze, the clay, the silver, and the gold—the great God has made known to the king what will come to pass after this. The dream is certain, and its interpretation is sure." Dan. 2:36–45

"For this is the covenant that I will make with the house of Israel after those days, says the Lord: I will put my laws in their mind and write them on their hearts; and I will be their God, and they shall be my people. None of them shall teach his neighbour, and none his brother, saying, 'Know the Lord,' for all shall know me, from the least of them to the greatest of them." Heb. 8:10-11

God set up a kingdom in which everyone will know him as he truly is. We must confess he is Lord in order to see his kingdom and enter into covenant with him. This is basic to being a Christian. Not only do we get to know him, but we also get to know him intimately as LORD.

Chapter 12: Grace

Grace is one of those words whose meaning has been modified and confused. Grace has taken on a whole personality of its own. It is one of the most over used and abused words in Christian lingo. The concept of grace is something that you may need to repent about. Repent means to change your perception or understanding to bring it in line with God's truth.

The first repentance - the one with the most impact - is when we repent about who Jesus is. We come into alignment with the truth that he is the Lord. This repentance initiates the steps that will lead us into God's kingdom. Repentance does not end there. It is something that will be required of us as we grow in our understanding of God and his Word. When God reveals his perspective of the truth, we repent of our previous thinking and align with his.

Jesus was full of grace and truth. That's where we start. "And the Word became flesh and dwelt among us, and we beheld His glory, the glory as of the only begotten of the Father, full of grace and truth." (John 1:14) Jesus was full of grace and truth. He never sinned. I mention the fact that he never sinned because some of us have been taught that grace forgives sin. Grace is given to help us obey, not to forgive sin.

Jesus was anointed. He was full of the Spirit. He was full of joy.

"That word you know, which was proclaimed throughout all Judea, and began from Galilee after the baptism which John preached: how God anointed Jesus of Nazareth with the Holy Spirit and with power, who went about doing good and healing all who were oppressed by the devil, for God was with Him." Acts 10:37–38

"You have loved righteousness and hated lawlessness; therefore God, Your God, has anointed You with the oil of gladness more than Your companions." Heb. 1:9

Jesus often said, "I tell you the truth..." What came next? You can do a study and search this out. The King James Version says, "Verily, verily I say unto you," - which is an old way of saying "I tell you the truth." Usually when Jesus draws attention to "truth" the next thing he will discuss is an aspect of the kingdom or government of God. Years ago we did a two year study on grace in the church I attended. Then I was asked to lead the church. I thought if Jesus was full of grace and truth maybe we should study truth for two years. So we did. It was in that study that I was lead into an understanding of the kingdom, because so many of the references Christ makes to truth are pointing to the kingdom.

Jesus was full of grace and truth. Grace and truth were partnered in Jesus. The current concepts of grace can include: kindness, graciousness, mercy, and forgiveness. When a lender extends grace it means you get more time to pay back the loan. Grace is also used for beautiful, fluid movement that one would see in ballet. Grace sounds like gracious which means "kind and courteous". Though they are similar in English, the two words are from different roots in the Greek language. Grace has a meaning in our culture that is different than the meaning in the Bible. We have used our culture's meaning of grace to interpret the Bible.

Grace is sort of contrasted with works in Ephesians 2:8–9. It almost seems that no work on our part is required. Grace must therefore mean "no work is required". Grace for many of us means to cut someone some slack. It means to allow a lower standard. It means to overlook flaws or faults. It means the opposite of being harsh or judgmental and the opposite of rigid legalistic compliance. Jesus was full of grace. Was God cutting him slack? Did he represent a lower standard?

The most common meaning of grace is - wait a minute! What do you think grace means? What kind of grace was Jesus full of? How do you define grace? Can you define it? Most often when I ask people to define grace they can't. Possibly they are intimidated or they are afraid of being wrong. Few volunteer an answer. What is your answer? Are you confident that it's right?

The most common definition for grace is unmerited favour. This definition is quite inadequate. "Unmerited" means undeserved and connotes to mercy. We think grace is mercy. Mercy is the motive behind grace but it is not grace. Mercy prompts you to give food to the poor. Food is what they need. They can't eat mercy. The food was the gift mercy provided. God in his mercy gives us grace.

Unmerited is an adjective and is less important to our understanding then the noun "favour". Think of a red car. What's more important, that it's red or that it's a car? Imagine talking to a member of some isolated tribe. You're trying to explain what a car is. Does the fact that it is red help? No. You must explain the noun. The adjective is not as important. We have not really understood what favour is so we have grabbed onto "unmerited" and derived a meaning that is close to, if not identical to, mercy.

What is favour? Favour is a synonym for grace. So the "unmerited favour" definition for grace means unmerited grace. Not a big help! The definition "unmerited favour" does not even come close to really explaining what grace is. All it does is spray paint a coat of mercy on favour. It gives favour the flavour of mercy.

A second problem with "unmerited" or "undeserved" is that many connote it to mean that nothing is required to get it. It does not convey accurately that we must do something to get grace. We don't earn it, but we have to do something to get it. God gives grace to the humble. So we have to be humble. Also, grace is accessed by faith, so we have to believe the promises of God to access grace.

Grace, in the New Testament, is the Greek word *charis*. Charis can also be translated joy or favour. As previously mentioned, grace is synonymous with favour. Grace is related to joy. They are the same in some instances. Charis is the first part of a word you may know - charisma. The Greek word *"charismata"* refers to the gifts of the Spirit. The gifts of the spirit are called the power gifts. That's a hint. Let's look at what the angel Gabriel said to Mary about favour when he stopped by for a chat in Luke 1:26–38 .

"Now in the sixth month the angel Gabriel was sent by God to a city of Galilee named Nazareth, to a virgin betrothed to a man whose name was Joseph, of the house of David. The virgin's name was Mary. And having come in, the angel said to her, 'Rejoice, highly favoured one, the Lord is with you; blessed are you among women!'

But when she saw him, she was troubled at his saying, and considered what manner of greeting this was. Then the angel said to her, 'Do not be afraid, Mary, for you have found favour with God. And behold, you will conceive in your womb and bring forth a Son, and shall call His name Jesus. He will be great, and will be called the Son of the Highest; and the Lord God will give Him the throne of His father David. And He will reign over the house of Jacob forever, and of His kingdom there will be no end.'

Then Mary said to the angel, 'How can this be, since I do not know a man?' And the angel answered and said to her, 'The Holy Spirit will come upon you, and the power of the Highest will overshadow you; therefore, also, that Holy One who is to be born will be called the Son of God. Now indeed, Elizabeth your relative has also conceived a son in her old age; and this is now the sixth month for her who was called barren. For with God nothing will be impossible.' Then Mary said, 'Behold the maidservant of the Lord! Let it be to me according to your word.' And the angel departed from her." Luke 1:26–38

This is a very interesting story, rich with meaning. I love this story. Imagine the Archangel Gabriel visiting you. Gabriel commands vast authority and power. He is a winged angel - a cherub. He most likely stands nine feet tall and glows in the dark. I kid you not. His presence inspires fear and terror. Notice how he says "Do not be afraid." When our children were small, one day we were singing a song with words that were, "though there be giants in the land I will not be afraid," at which point our four year old piped up "I will be afraid." You have to love the honesty of a four year old. Yes, if a nine foot tall winged angel appeared it would make me afraid.

Gabriel told Mary she was favoured. Mary was favoured by God. You could say she was graced by God. The archangel greeted her with these words:

1) You are highly favoured.
2) The Lord is with you.
3) Blessed are you.
(The word "blessed" means empowered to prosper.)

Gabriel went on to explain the details of the favour she was blessed with. She was told that she would do the impossible - bear a child while being virgin. Not just any child - God's child. How was this going to happen? How was the favour to unfold? The favour was that the Holy Spirit would come upon her and the **power** of God would create life.

> Grace is the empowering presence of God.
> Grace is the Holy Spirit.
> Grace is joy unspeakable.

Grace is divine strength, divine power, divine energy, and divine effort.
Grace is God doing the work.

A verse that confirms this is 2 Cor. 12:9. Paul understood grace. Grace is divine strength and power.

> "And He said to me, 'My **grace** is sufficient for you, for my **strength** is made perfect in weakness.' Therefore most gladly I will rather boast in my infirmities, that the **power** of Christ may rest upon me." (2 Cor. 12:9)

The new covenant is called a covenant of grace. What's different about the new covenant is that God has poured out his Spirit - his grace - his enabling power upon believers so that they can do the same works Jesus did. Jesus was full of grace and truth. He was full of grace - the oil (Spirit) of gladness, the power of the Spirit, divine strength - and truth. The Holy Spirit is grace to us.

The covenant of grace is not a covenant with lower standards. Jesus made that clear in Matthew 5 when he said that to enter the kingdom of God your righteousness must exceed the righteousness of the Pharisees. He said the law says "Do not murder," but I say "do not hate". The law says "Do not commit adultery," but I say "do not lust". The new covenant has higher standards than the old. The new covenant has impossible standards.

The old covenant relied on human effort (works of the flesh). People had to obey using their own strength. **Trying to obey the law with human effort or work is called the system of the law** or legalism. In the new covenant, God supplies the power needed to comply with his standards in the person of the Holy Spirit. You became part of the new covenant by the work done for you by God. Jesus did the work that saved you. You can add nothing to his effort. His effort totally suffices. You are saved by putting faith in Him and the work he did on your behalf. You were dead in trespasses of sin and He made you alive. It takes energy to raise someone from the dead.

"But God, who is rich in mercy, because of His great love with which He loved us, even when we were dead in trespasses, made us alive together with Christ (by grace you have been saved), and raised us up together, and made us sit together in the heavenly places in Christ Jesus, that in the ages to come He might show the exceeding riches of His grace in His kindness toward us in Christ Jesus. For by grace you have been saved through faith, and that not of yourselves; it is the gift of God, not of works, lest anyone should boast. For we are His workmanship, created in Christ Jesus for good works, which God prepared beforehand that we should walk in them." Eph. 2:4–10

This passage tells us that God loves us with a great love. It tells us that his mercy motivated him to use his own power to make us alive. For by grace (divine effort) you have been saved, not of works (human effort). We are created to do good works. The good works are not works done in human effort but works done using the power of the Holy Spirit. They are not works done to earn salvation but works done by one already saved and part of the family.

The new covenant is called a covenant of grace. That grace is in the Holy Spirit. The only way we should operate in the new covenant is by using his power, not our own. Burn the oil, not the wick. Isn't it time we learned to operate using his power?

Law and Grace

> "For the law was given through Moses, but grace and truth came through Jesus Christ." John 1:17

This verse seems to be contrasting law with grace, as if grace is the opposite of law. In the Greek language this verse actually says, "Because the law through Moses was given, grace and truth through Jesus became." (John 1:17 Greek transliteration) The Greek shows cause and effect. The verse before this says, "And of His fullness we have all received, and grace for grace."(John 1:16) It means we have received one gift of grace after another, first the law, then grace and truth. It's weird that the law should be called a gift of grace but think about it. Grace is power. God's Word contains power. "For the Word of God is living and powerful." (Heb. 4:12)

"And with great power the apostles gave witness to the resurrection of the Lord Jesus. And great grace was upon them all." Acts 4:33 Notice the use of "power" and "grace". They are synonymous.

"For sin shall not have dominion (power to control) over you, for you are not under law (the system of law powered by human effort) but under grace (divine power). What then? Shall we sin because we are not under law but under grace? Certainly not!" Rom. 6:15–16 {God's power enables us to overcome sin.}

"I became a minister according to the gift of the **grace** of God given to me by the effective working of His **power**." Eph. 3:7

Grace is power. Grace is Holy Spirit power.

> "And He said to me, 'My **grace** is sufficient for you, for my **strength** is made perfect in weakness.' Therefore most gladly I will rather boast in my infirmities, that the **power** of Christ may rest upon me." (2 Cor. 12:9)

A Musing 13: Covenant of Grace

Did you ever stop to consider that in the covenant we have through Christ Jesus, that what God said to Mary also applies to us?

> You are highly favoured.
> The Lord is with you.
> Blessed are you.

The Old Testament prayer from Numbers 6:24–26, "The Lord bless you and keep you; The Lord make his face to shine towards you and be gracious to you; The Lord lift up his countenance upon you and give you peace", is for us. The actual words God chooses to have us pray are packed with meaning.

Bless means to empower to prosper in five areas.

1) health
2) financially (personal and business)
3) fecundity (having healthy babies, fruitful)
4) spiritually
5) socially

God is committed to our success.

The Lord bless you (prosper you) and keep you (protect you); The Lord make his face to shine towards you (smile upon you) and be gracious to you (show you covenant kindness); The Lord lift up his countenance upon you (smile again) and give you peace (prosperity and all the benefits of the cross). (Expanded version of Num. 6:24-26)

A Musing 14: Ternopil

I have been to Ternopil in the Ukraine twice to teach. When I say Ternopil, people sometimes think I mean Chernobyl. I'm not saying "Chernobyl" though I wonder if they have a Woman's Aglow there. I'm saying Ternopil. I taught for two weeks at a seminary in Ternopil. I spent most of the time teaching on the government of God, but I finished with some teaching about grace. The Eastern Block people already have so much government, why give them more? Well because the kingdom is not more government. It is good government.

It is important, if we are to function in God's government, that we understand grace. May I say that some of the churches in the Ukraine maybe lean a bit towards joyless legalism? Their music is really beautiful but very melancholy. One evening I shared with the class of over one hundred seminary students about grace. I asked them, "Are you sinners or are you saved by grace?" One grey haired old farmer proffered that he was a sinner saved by grace.

I responded that a sinner is outside the family of God; under the wrath of God; he will die and go to Hell. A person saved by grace is adopted into the family of God; he is accepted in the beloved; his sins are washed away; and his destiny is eternity in the presence of God. A person saved by grace is set apart for God. He is a saint (someone set apart for God). You are either one or the other - a sinner or a saint. I saw it in his eyes - the grey haired farmer - the lights went on. He understood. He is a new creature in Christ. I love it when the lights go on. How do you see yourself - a sinner or a saint?

Chapter 13: Joy

The kingdom of God is righteousness and peace and **joy**. Kingdom of God means government of God or rule of Christ. The rule of Christ, which is vastly superior to the rule of sin, is righteousness, peace and joy in Christ - the Holy Spirit.

Righteousness means doing right. We know this from the context of Rom. 14:17–18 because it is talking about **serving** Christ. If the context was justification, then righteousness in this passage would mean right standing. Right standing is gift from Jesus and precedes right doing. Right doing means we obey God - we obey his word and we obey his Spirit. He is our Lord.

Peace includes all the benefits of complete salvation and covenant living. It means we have access to all that belongs to the Father. We have access to Heaven's resources. Peace means healing and health, prosperity and all the benefits of the cross. Peace means we are fully equipped with his resources to serve God where and when he wants.

Joy is wonderful! Joy means we don't have to serve God in our own strength. The joy of the Lord is our strength. In the presence of the Lord is fulness of joy. God is always with us. His presence goes with us. He will not abandon us. Joy links strength and presence. Joy is just like grace. Grace means divine empowerment. Joy means divine strength. The two concepts are very similar. You could even say they are the same. We can come boldly to the throne of grace - which is where God resides. The throne of grace is in his presence and that's where his joy becomes our strength. Joy means we can serve God using his power.

Righteousness has for too long been linked to legalistic requirements. True righteousness is not legalistic. We should love righteousness. Jesus did. And it brought him joy. "You have loved righteousness and hated lawlessness; therefore God, your God, has anointed you with the oil of gladness more than your companions." (Heb. 1:9)

When we operate with joy we are actually carrying the presence of God. Perhaps it would be just as accurate to say the presence carries us. We want to be in his presence. We want his Spirit to be upon us like a dove. We don't want to scare away the dove. We don't want to get into trying to please God through our own efforts alone. Yes, some effort on our part is required, but that effort is to focus on him - to trust him. We are to walk in love and we are to be joyful. Obeying God in his grace is a joy because he does the work. And his work is to preach the kingdom, open blind eyes, heal the sick, free the oppressed and raise the dead. What could be simpler? In his presence all things are possible.

Chapter 14: On Earth

> "Thy Kingdom come, thy will be done on earth as
> it is in Heaven." Matt. 6:10

In Heaven there is no sorrow; there is no pain; no death.
In Heaven there is no sickness or disease.
In Heaven there is no anxiety, no deception, no depression, and no addiction.
In Heaven there is no want - no poverty.
In Heaven there is joy. There is peace. There is love.
In Heaven there is happy surrender to the will of God.
In Heaven there is a Lord, who sits on a throne and is acknowledged as ruler over all.

For many in the church, past and present, the focus has been to prepare to escape earth and to go to Heaven. Jesus didn't teach us to bide our time until we die and go to Heaven. He wanted us to bring Heaven to earth. All of creation is waiting for the sons of God to be revealed. Who are the sons of God? They are the mature offspring of God who reflect His nature and power in the earth.

> "For the earnest expectation of the creation
> eagerly waits for the revealing of the sons (huios)
> of God." Rom. 8:19

> "For as many as are led by the Spirit of God, these
> are sons (huios) of God." Rom. 8:14

"Sons" is a translation of the Greek New Testament word "huios". Huios means "mature son that reflects the nature of his father". A different Greek word is used for the newly converted. It is teknon. The Greek language differentiates between a born-again believer (teknon) and grown-up born-again believer (huios). For our purposes and throughout this book, huios is not gender specific. Just like the bride of Christ includes males, the "sons" of God includes females. So whenever I use the pronoun "he" or "his" in reference to huios please understand it includes "she" and "her".

Two things distinguish a mature son of God.

1) He is governed by God. He is led of the Spirit. He knows the Lord. He hears and obeys. This is the inward component of the kingdom.

2) He goes about healing the sick and preaching the kingdom of God. He is like Jesus – "doing good, healing all who are oppressed by the devil." He demonstrates and proclaims the kingdom of God. This is the outward component of the kingdom.

Almost all Christians today are teknons. They have the seed of the Father. They are born-again. They are redeemed. It is a great thing to be a teknon. It is a great thing to be saved from sin and be Heaven bound. But creation is not eagerly waiting for the revealing of the teknons of God. Creation is not in earnest expectation of seeing another teknon. Quite frankly creation is bored with seeing teknons. It is not overly impressed with them.

Teknons are believers but they are not mature like Jesus. Jesus was never called the Teknon of God but always the Huios of God. Jesus did the will of the Father in the power of the Spirit. Creation wants to see Him again. Creation wants to see more sons modelled after the Huios of God. Will you be one of them?

Review of the Greek words:

Teknon:

> Born-again legal offspring
> Adopted into the family of God
> A saint - set apart for God
> Needs milk of the Word
> Needs to be made into a disciple
> Needs to mature
> Needs to learn how to serve

Huios:

> Mature teknon that reflects the nature of the Father
> Does the works of Jesus in the power of the Spirit
> and in the will of the Father
> Heals the sick, raises the dead, opens blind eyes
> Casts out evil spirits, preaches the kingdom of God
> Serves God using divine energy not human effort
> Hears and obeys the Spirit

"For the earnest expectation of the creation eagerly waits for the revealing of the huios of God." Rom. 8:19 The "revealing" has already started! There are men and women today that are stepping up and becoming huios. They are embracing true sonship. They are "doing the stuff", as John Wimber used to say. "Doing the stuff" means healing the sick and using the gifts of the Spirit in evangelism. There are leaders who are equipping the saints to do the work of the ministry. There are leaders who are modelling, for the rest of us, the importance of being led of the Spirit. That, dear reader, is very cool.

Still, there are many in the body of Christ that don't know how to do the stuff, or even know there is stuff to do. There are many who have not grown beyond being teknons. There are many who have not been equipped to hear and obey the Spirit. That is about to change.

The whole earth will be filled with the knowledge of His glory as the waters cover the sea. Do you want to mature from teknon to huios? Do you want to become Spirit-led? Do you want to work like Jesus did - healing the sick and casting out demons? Do you want to "see the Father" and know what he is saying and doing? I hope you do and I hope this short look into becoming huios will assist you in your journey. I hope this book will serve as a manual to prepare you to join the growing number of believers that creation is eagerly waiting for.

"Thy Kingdom come, Thy will be done on earth as it is in Heaven." Matt. 6:10

A Musing 15: The Five Fold Ministry

Over the years there has been much said about the five-fold ministry. We have tried to define what apostles are and what they are called to do. Different opinions abound but there is one thing I think that we can all agree on. Let's read the passage from Ephesians first.

"And He Himself gave some to be apostles, some prophets, some evangelists, and some pastors and teachers, <u>for the equipping of the saints for the work of ministry</u>, for the edifying of the body of Christ, till we all come to the unity of the faith and of the knowledge of the Son of God, to a perfect man, to the measure of the stature of the fullness of Christ; that we should no longer be children, tossed to and fro and carried about with every wind of doctrine, by the trickery of men, in the cunning craftiness of deceitful plotting, but, speaking the truth in love, may grow up in all things into Him who is the head, Christ, from whom the whole body, joined and knit together by what every joint supplies, according to the effective working by which every part does its share, causes growth of the body for the edifying of itself in love." Eph. 4:11–16

Jesus gave us the Fabulous Five - apostles, prophets, evangelists, pastors and teachers - to do the work of the ministry. Is that right? Wait! Is that what you read? Back up! The fabulous five were given to equip the saints (people in the pews) to do the work of the ministry. So no matter what the different opinions are on the various functions of the five-fold, one function is clear. They should be equipping us to do the work of ministry. And that is not happening much.

There are a few churches and revival centres equipping the saints and it seems that it may be on the increase. I have heard teaching on the five-fold for forty years, starting with Restoration teaching from Bible Temple and it is only recently that equipping the saints to do the work is really coming of age.

If you read the passage above you will see the goal of God in giving the five-fold is to produce huios. "May grow up", "no longer children", "perfect (complete) man" and "fulness of Christ" are ideas pointing to the concept of turning teknon into huios. The five-fold have a job to do. They are to coach and develop ordinary saints, like you and me, into ministers. Ministers are servants. We are to learn how to **serve** in the government of God. "For the kingdom of God is not eating and drinking, but righteousness and peace and joy in the Holy Spirit. For he who **serves** Christ in these things is acceptable to God and approved by men." (Rom. 14:17–18)

The growth into maturity does not take place in the pews. It takes place in the community as we minister reconciliation in the marketplace and in homes. We heal the sick and cast out demons and preach the good news of the government of God. Becoming huios is more than an academic exercise. It cannot be learned in classrooms or lecture halls. Ministry is not the profession of a chosen few but the purpose of the whole body of Christ. How are we to minister? Who are we to minister to?

It occurs to me, that if regular little ol' you and me are to be equipped to minister effectively then one thing would be really handy. It would be good to know the leading of the Spirit. Jesus only did what he saw the Father doing. Don't you agree, that part of the equipping process should be to model, impart, and teach how to operate in the Spirit - how to hear and obey the Spirit? I mean, I can't heal anyone but Christ in me can. I can't raise people from the dead but the same Spirit that raised Jesus from the dead dwells in me. He can do it. I need to be huios to do the works of Jesus and the huios of God are led of the Spirit. "For as many as are led by the Spirit of God, these are huios of God." (Rom. 8:14)

Should we be giving the saints opportunity to pray for the sick and learn to operate in the gifts of the Spirit? Should we allow time in our meetings to practice skills? Or is sitting passively in a pew going to produce a victorious church? Maybe it is time we nicely asked those that call themselves "five-fold" to equip **us** to do the work. We could say, "I really appreciate your sermons, but I want some hands on experience. Let's go to the hospital or mortuary this afternoon and you can show me how you heal the sick and raise the dead."

They are doing that in Redding, California at Bethel Church. You should read Kevin Dedmon's book *The Ultimate Treasure Hunt*. He tells how church members are taking healing into the community. Randy Clark from Global Awakening gives opportunity for believers to go to Brazil and other places to be part of ministry teams. I got excellent hands on experience operating in words of knowledge and praying for the sick when I was with him in Brazil. It was amazing seeing people I prayed for getting healed. Mind you, I had to learn to pray in Portuguese. *Mais Senhor!* (More Lord!)

It is perhaps time we structured church meetings to better accommodate equipping the saints and teaching them how to hear the Spirit accurately. The goal of every believer should be to walk in the Spirit - to become huios. The kingdom of God is the rule of Christ. It is obvious to me that the role of true leadership in the body of Christ is to instruct, facilitate and activate church members to hear and obey the Spirit personally. What could be more vital?

"That word you know, which was proclaimed throughout all Judea, and began from Galilee after the baptism which John preached: how God **anointed** Jesus of Nazareth **with the Holy Spirit and with power**, who went about doing good and healing all who were oppressed by the devil, for God was with Him." Acts 10:37–38

The Restoration movement tried to heighten our awareness of the five-fold ministry but these five-fold ministers did little more than do some entertaining teaching from the pulpit. They are supposed to be coaches putting us on the field. It's time for leaders to stop ministering to the saints and start equipping them to minister. We need to forge passive members into an effective army of fully equipped, Spirit-empowered and Spirit-led huios. All of creation is waiting.

Chapter 15: The Will of God

> "Thy Kingdom come, thy will be done on earth as it is in Heaven." Matt. 6:10

The first thing that comes to my mind when I read the phrase "will of God" is the idea of inheriting. The reading of the will usually means we are about to benefit in some way. It is my hope that at the reading of some relative's will, I will inherit a condo in Maui. The last chapter introduced the idea that where God's will is done there is no sickness, no sorrow, and no pain. When God's will is done we inherit the benefits of his desire for us. God's will is good. When we follow his commands as in, do his will, good results.

Imagine if you will that everyone obeyed the command not to steal. Would that make life better or worse? You wouldn't need theft insurance for your car or home. Stores wouldn't have to factor theft into the retail price and prices would go down. Locksmiths and the people who install alarm systems might not like it, but most other lives would be better. Maybe when God told us not to steal he wanted us to inherit a bit of Heaven.

The Law Is a Delight

"Blessed is the man who walks not in the counsel of the ungodly, nor stands in the path of sinners, nor sits in the seat of the scornful; but his **delight is in the law of the Lord**, and in His law he meditates day and night. He shall be like a tree planted by the rivers of water, which brings forth its fruit in its season, whose leaf also shall not wither; and whatever he does shall prosper." Ps. 1:1–3

We need to see doing his will, obeying his commands and aligning with his kingdom as a really good thing. We need to see his law as a delight. "I delight to do your will, O my God, and your law is within my heart." (Ps. 40:8) Paul wrote, "For I **delight** in the law of God according to the inward man." (Rom. 7:22) Paul was writing in the New Testament from a new covenant perspective. There are those that argue that Romans 7 is alluding to a time before Paul knew Christ. I don't buy that theory. In Rom. 8:7 (which according to that theory it would be after Paul knew Christ) Paul continues - "the carnal mind is enmity against God for it is not subject to the law of God." Paul, in the context of the new covenant considered it carnal **not** to be subject to God's law.

"Then I said, 'Behold, I have come — in the volume of the book it is written of me — to do your will, O God.'" Heb. 10:7 (Referring to Jesus)

We have to disassociate the law of God with the restrictions of legalism and build a new association to the law - that of bringing heaven to earth. Legalism is the "system of the law". It is trying to do God's will with human effort. The new covenant makes legalism obsolete because the new covenant provides grace - divine power to obey his will and bring his inheritance to earth.

The Law Is Written On Our Hearts

> "For this is the covenant that I will make with the house of Israel after those days, says the Lord: <u>I will put my laws in their mind and write them on their hearts</u>; and I will be their God, and they shall be my people." Heb. 8:10

The very basis of the new covenant is that we know God's laws. It's right there in Heb. 8:10. God's laws are instructions. The word "laws" in this passage is not referring to the system of the law where one had to work (in the power of human flesh) to attain righteousness. In this instance "laws" is his inspired Word. His Word reveals his will.

When I align my will with God's will, I align with Heaven. I align with Heaven's peace, with Heaven's resources, with Heaven's power, with Heaven's health, with Heaven's protection, with Heaven's joy. My wise heavenly Father, who knows best, and who is committed to my success - my health, my happiness - who is for me and with me, tells me to do something. Is that command a burden or a path to my inheritance? When I willingly submit to the government of heaven will I be robbed or enriched?

When God gives us a command it is for our own good. It is life to us. We should respond to his command with a willingness to do it. We should ask him for his help to do it. We should partner with him to do it. We should say, "God, I want to do your will. Please fill me with your joy so I can." We should turn every command into an adventure of seeing what he is going do in and through us. We should relate to his commands in a positive and intimate way. He expects us to obey. He expects us to obey using his strength, not our own. He expects us to succeed. He loves us and is committed to our success. He guides us into truth. Truth sets us free. His commands are what we need to prosper.

Those who delight in the law of God prosper.

"For I have not spoken on my own authority; but the Father who sent me gave me a command, what I should say and what I should speak. And I know that His command is everlasting life. Therefore, whatever I speak, just as the Father has told me, so I speak." John 12:49–50

Jesus said doing the command of God was life to him. Jesus delighted to do the will of the Father. Pray with me..."Father I pray that doing your will, will become my delight. I ask in Jesus' name."

Jesus wants his followers to experience divine life. That's why he said, "teaching them to observe all things that I have commanded you; and lo, I am with you always," (Matt. 28:20). His commands bring us into life. Obeying his commands is a way into his presence. His presence is a way into further obedience. We can obey because he is with us always. Pray with me..."Father, help me to spend more time in your presence."

A Musing 16: The Heart

> "I will put my laws in their mind and write them
> on their **hearts**." Heb. 8:10

Why does God put his law in our mind and write it on our heart? Why two places? We know that the original covenant terms were written on two tablets of stone. Did you know that the custom in those days was to make a copy of the terms for each person in the covenant? Then each one would go to his own home with his copy. God gave his copy to Moses. He was in a sense saying to Moses "I will dwell with you and the people of Israel." That speaks to the fact that God dwells among us. He will never leave us or forsake us. That is very cool. But why are there two internal copies of the law given to us?

Just for clarity - God is not putting the "system of the law" into our minds. He is putting his Word into our minds. The Old Testament was written to teach us. "All Scripture is given by inspiration of God, and is profitable for doctrine, for reproof, for correction, for instruction in righteousness, that the man of God may be complete, thoroughly equipped for every good work." (2 Tim. 3:16–17) So we get the law or Word itself, not the system of the law. Remember the law is good, but working the law as a system is bad. God writes his scripture on our heart and puts it in our mind.

We know what the mind is. Most everyone you meet has one. The mind resides in the brain. What is the heart and where does it reside? What does the Bible say?

Prov. 23:7   "For as he thinks in his heart, so is he."

Matt. 12:34   "For out of the abundance of the heart the mouth speaks."

Matt. 12:35   "A good man out of the good <u>treasure</u> of his heart brings forth good things, and an evil man out of the evil treasure brings forth evil things."

According to the Bible the heart is an organ of thought, the source of speech and a repository of memory. The Bible is not talking about the muscle in your chest that pumps blood. The muscle in your chest that pumps blood is, in fact, a muscle in your chest that pumps blood. So if you get a heart transplant it doesn't upset the repository of memory or where God has written his law.

The word "heart" in the Bible means inner core. It refers to a deep place that cannot be seen. In function it is similar to the mind in that it is the source of thought and speech and God can write on it. It is most likely what modern science refers to as the subconscious mind. It resides in the brain. The subconscious contains memories. It uses those memories to **filter** new things, sounds and ideas. It tells us what to pay attention to and what to ignore. You're in a meeting, and in the next room a baby cries - you ignore it - but its mommy jumps up and runs into the next room. Your filter said, "Not important." Mommy's filter said, "Red alert! All hands on deck!"

The subconscious is programmed by repetition or by a highly impacting event. The event can be good - in the case of being baptized in the Spirit, or it can be bad - as in the case of being shot. Your subconscious mind's hard drive had some lines of code rewritten when the Spirit was first invited in. Normally it is reprogrammed by repetition. Things that get repeated over and over again over time are called traditions. The traditions of men make the Word of none effect. They program our subconscious into a bad filter. The Word of God programs our subconscious into a good filter. "Your word I have hidden in my heart that I might not sin against you." Ps. 119:11

"This Book of the Law shall not depart from your mouth, but you shall meditate in it day and night, that you may observe to do according to all that is written in it. For then you will make your way prosperous, and then you will have good success." Josh. 1:8

"And these words which I command you today shall be in your heart. You shall teach them diligently to your children, and shall talk of them when you sit in your house, when you walk by the way, when you lie down, and when you rise up. You shall bind them as a sign on your hand, and they shall be as frontlets (forehead bands between your eyes). You shall write them on the doorposts of your house and on your gates." Deut. 6:6–9

The Old Testament was written to teach us. "All Scripture is given by inspiration of God, and is profitable for doctrine, for reproof, for correction, for instruction in righteousness, that the man of God may be complete, thoroughly equipped for every good work." (2 Tim. 3:16–17) The way God writes his law in our hearts is through the repetition of hearing, reading, meditating, and memorizing the Word. The way God writes his law in our hearts is through the repetition of hearing, reading, meditating, and memorizing the Word. The way...

Wouldn't it be nice if God just gave us an instant download? I suspect that might interfere in a small way with free will. We must partner with God to have his word dwell in us richly. We must make an effort to reprogram our subconscious with the Word of God. God is looking for heart faith. We must confess with our mouth that Jesus is Lord and believe in our heart, for it is with the heart confession is made unto salvation.

The Centurion had heart faith. It came about as he repeatedly saw servants and soldiers obey him day after day. He got used to it. His heart expected it. Faith is the expectation of things hoped for.

The heart is the subconscious mind and is programmed by repetition. God writes his law in our hearts and puts it in our minds. His law must be valuable. "Therefore the law is holy, and the commandment holy and just and good." Rom. 7:12

Chapter 16: The Tree of Life

"And he showed me a pure river of water of life, clear as crystal, proceeding from the throne of God and of the Lamb. In the middle of its street, and on either side of the river, was the tree of life, which bore twelve fruits, each tree yielding its fruit every month. The leaves of the tree were for the healing of the nations. And there shall be no more curse, but the throne of God and of the Lamb shall be in it, and His servants shall serve Him. They shall see His face, and His name shall be on their foreheads. There shall be no night there: They need no lamp nor light of the sun, for the Lord God gives them light. And they shall reign forever and ever." Rev. 22:1–5

"Blessed are those who do His commandments that they may have the right to the tree of life, and may enter through the gates into the city. But outside are dogs and sorcerers and sexually immoral and murderers and idolaters, and whoever loves and practices a lie." Rev. 22:14–15

The tree of life is mentioned in the second chapter of the first book of the Bible. It is mentioned again in the closing chapter of the last book of the Bible. Adam and Eve disobeyed God and were removed from the Garden of Eden. They were denied access to the tree of life. Remember that their sin did not separate them from the love of God. It did, however, separate them from the life of God. They started to die from that point onwards. Jesus spoke these words, "I am the way, the truth and the life." (John 14:6) Jesus came to restore access to the tree of life.

What is the setting of Revelation chapter 22 and where are we in the picture? We see the river of life. We see the throne of God. We see the Lamb. Where are we? Oh! There we are – "His servants will serve him." We find that we are called servants.

I believe that we are called to be huios of God. Creation is waiting for the revealing of the huios of God. I believe that when we are born again we become his children (teknon). God is our Father. I also believe we are called to be servants. Servants are those who have aligned with the will of God. They obey his commands. They are blessed with access to the tree of life. "Blessed are those who do His commandments, that they may have the right to the tree of life." Rev. 22:14

Jesus set the example for us to follow. He did his Father's commands (John 12:49). They were everlasting life to him. Jesus was a huios. He was in fact the Huios. He was also a servant. "Now, Lord, look on their threats, and grant to your servants that with all boldness they may speak your word, by stretching out your hand to heal, and that signs and wonders may be done through the name of your holy Servant Jesus." (Acts 4:29–30) The disciples were also servants. The writers of the Epistles called themselves bondservants. The early church knew that they served God. We too are servants.

The purpose of obeying the commands of God is to bring us into life. The purpose is to bless. Bless means to empower to prosper. By serving we learn to reign. The enemy wants us to think that serving God and obeying his commands will bring us into legalism and death. The enemy wants us to think the only way to serve and obey is by legalism. The enemy is a liar. Legalism is not God's path. It is man's pride.

Legalism is saying to God that I can do it myself. I can merit your love. Legalism is the tree of death. Pride is the author of legalism. It is contrary to the ways of God. We have to sever the concept of obedience from the concept of earning our way into Heaven. The way of serving is open to blood-bought Bible-taught Spirit-filled born-again believers.

We are talking of the post-saved not the pre-saved. We serve and obey because we are saved. And we serve so we can experience life. His servants shall serve him. It is an honour to serve God. It is an honour to follow the example given by the holy servant Jesus.

Is the passage from Revelation 22 speaking of Heaven or is it on Earth? Here's a thought you may want to consider. If the leaves of the tree of life are for the healing of nations, then maybe the venue is not the afterlife but the life we are now living. The servants can enter the city of God. Maybe the servants of the Lord have access to the tree of life so that they can procure what is needed by people here on earth. The fruit of the tree of life is available year round. In other words, God's resources are always accessible. God gives his servants light. There is no night for them. They can reign even in darkness because they have an eternal source of light and provision. They have the ability to change the environment in which they live. They have the ability to reign over darkness, sickness, and poverty.

Serving God is a good thing. Servants see God's face. His name is on their foreheads. We are called to serve from a place of intimacy with our Lord. His commands are life to us.

Pray with me... "Father, help me to be your servant. Help me to do your will. Help me to come into your city to get resources to serve you here on earth. Help me to bring heaven to earth. Thy will be done on earth as it is in Heaven. I ask in Jesus' name."

What gives us access to the tree of life? "Blessed are those who do His commandments, that they may have the right to the tree of life." (Rev. 22:14)

A Musing 17: Unravelling Revelation

This musing is completely crazy yet at the same time quite fascinating. It's sparked by the fact we were just in Revelation and I remarked that perhaps the venue might not be the afterlife, but the here and now. There are many different points of view when it comes to Revelation.

I read a very interesting perspective recently. If you want to have some intrigue, google James Stuart Russell's *The Parousia*. There is a free download of his entire book available. Be prepared. It was first published in 1878 and the author is articulate and erudite. You may need a dictionary. His ideas are controversial. They may take you out of your comfort zone.

James Russell looks at Matthew 24 and the Book of Revelation in considerable detail. He shows how the Epistles and other books speak of the imminent return of Christ. Let's read a bit of Revelation to give you the idea.

"The Revelation of Jesus Christ, which God gave Him to show His servants - things which must shortly take place. And He sent and signified it by His angel to His servant John, who bore witness to the word of God, and to the testimony of Jesus Christ, to all things that he saw. Blessed is he who reads and those who hear the words of this prophecy, and keep those things which are written in it; for the time is near." Rev. 1:1–3

> "He who testifies to these things says, "Surely I am coming quickly." Amen. Even so, come, Lord Jesus!" Rev. 22:20

What if Rev. 1:1-3 is the key to understanding the entire book? What if the underlined words are true? What if "Behold I stand at the door and knock," (Rev. 3:20) meant I'm practically on your doorstep? The book of Revelation starts and ends with the thought of his imminent return. I looked up imminent in the dictionary and was shocked to find it did not say - a 2000 year period of time. {Imminent: - likely to occur at any moment; impending; menacingly near or at hand.}

What happened in 70 AD?

It's something to ponder.

Chapter 17: The Way, the Truth and the Life

"For in Him dwells all the fullness of the Godhead bodily." Col. 2:9

Jesus is the visible representation of the godhead. God chose that all fulness would dwell in Jesus. Jesus is the king of the kingdom. The kingdom of God centres on the Lord Jesus. God has given Jesus a name which is above every name - Lord. The Father gave Jesus his own name. The full name and title of Jesus is the Lord Jesus Christ. You could also say Lord Jesus the Christ. Lord is his first name. Jesus is his second name and Christ is his title. Christ means the anointed one or the Messiah. Jesus means Saviour. Lord means master/owner or "he who must be obeyed." Jesus is the mediator between man and God. The way, the truth, and the life represent his tri-fold function representing the Godhead.

The **way** is the way of righteousness. It is doing the will of the Father. The **truth** is that you can have access to heaven's resources. The truth will set you free from sickness, poverty and oppression. The truth will save you. The **life** is in the Spirit. The life is in the Presence. We saw all three aspects of kingdom life in the passages from Rev. 22:1–5.

We saw that we were servants. That means we have aligned with the Lordship of Jesus. We are prepared to obey his commands because we have been bought with a price - the blood of Jesus, and we belong to him. We are walking in love. Love is a commitment to do what is righteous. Servants do the will of the master.

We saw that we had access to Heaven's resources - fruit and leaves. The leaves are for healing. The fruit is available all twelve months of the year. We are to heal the sick and preach the kingdom. Heaven provides all that we need to accomplish our mission. There is no more curse - just blessings.

The servants were in the throne room. They were in the presence of God. God sits on a throne, not a sofa. Grace sits on a throne. The throne is a kingdom concept. The servants get to rule and reign with Christ. They see the face of God. They have the name of God on their forehead. They belong to God. They have access to the throne. They can come boldly into his presence with reverence. The Lord gives them light. "In him was life and the life was the light of men." (John 1:4) There is life in the Presence and we carry the Presence with us - Christ in us the hope of glory.

Is it important that we know Jesus as Lord? Is it important that we follow his example of hearing and obeying the Father? Is it important that we understand that we are servants as well as sons? Yes. Yes. Yes. The kingdom of God is in the Holy Spirit and those that serve Christ are acceptable to God. (Rom. 14:18) Servants get to rule and reign in life.

Chapter 18: Renewing our Mind

We are born again in a four step process, similar in some ways to entering into a marriage covenant. Our covenant is primarily a covenant of love, and the government of God is best seen as a family structure not a corporation. God is both Lord and love.

Marriage consists of four steps:

1) attraction
2) decision
3) ceremony
4) consummation

These four steps are symbolic of coming under new management in a four step process called the new birth. The four steps are as follows:

1) repentance
2) faith
3) immersion in water
4) immersion in the Spirit

God was not happy with the Mosaic covenant because the people failed to uphold it. In the new covenant he writes his laws in our hearts and minds instead of two tablets of stone. Those laws are his teachings which we then mix with grace (his power) in order to fulfil them.

We are not under law in the sense of a path to righteousness and we are not under the system of the law which is a legalistic attempt to obey God in human strength alone. We are under a new system - that of grace - whereby we are enriched and empowered by the indwelling Spirit to do the will of God in His strength. We delight in the law of God in the sense that as born-again saints, we want to be great in the kingdom or government of God.

"For assuredly, I say to you, till heaven and earth pass away, one jot or one tittle will by no means pass from the law till all is fulfilled. Whoever therefore breaks one of the least of these commandments, and teaches men so, shall be called least in the kingdom of heaven; but whoever does and teaches them, <u>he shall be called great in the kingdom of heaven</u>." Matt 5:18–19

Grace means divine power, not just unmerited favour. It means the power of God as supplied by the indwelling Holy Spirit. It relates to the joy of his presence. In his presence is fullness of joy and that joy is our strength. Grace is a word synonymous with divine strength and power as evidenced in Paul's writings. "And He said to me, "My <u>grace</u> is sufficient for you, for my <u>strength</u> is made perfect in weakness." Therefore most gladly I will rather boast in my infirmities, that the <u>power of Christ</u> may rest upon me." (2 Cor. 12:9)

Those who delight in the law of God prosper and those that obey the commands of God have access to the tree of life. We have been bought with a price and must use our bodies as instruments of righteousness. We are servants of the Lord and well as children of the Father.

Heaven is a wonderful place and when we align with God's government we gain access to heaven's resources - wisdom, health and wealth. "Thy kingdom come thy will be done on earth as it is in Heaven," (Matt. 6:10) means we can bring Heaven to earth.

Chapter 19: The Super Blessing

As a born again believer in the Lord Jesus, you have been redeemed from the curse and have inherited the blessings of Abraham. You have all the benefits of the cross. You have peace.

Benefits of the Cross: (extract from *Understanding the Kingdom of God*)

1. Jesus was punished that we might be forgiven.

2. Jesus was wounded that we might be healed. Is. 53:4–5 reveals that Jesus bore the consequences of our sin both in the spiritual and the physical sense. Our sins are forgiven and our sickness is healed. (See 1 Peter 1:24)

3. Jesus was made sin with our sinfulness that we might become righteous with His righteousness. "For God made Jesus who knew no sin to be sin for us that we might become the righteousness of God in Him." (2 Cor. 5:21)

4. Jesus died our death that we might share His life. "Jesus tasted death for everyone." (Heb. 2:9) (See Rom. 6:23)

5. Jesus became poor with our poverty that we might become rich with His riches. "…That you through His poverty might become rich." (2 Cor. 8:9) While Jesus walked this earth he was not poor. He had all that He needed to do the will of God in his own life. On the cross, Jesus was hungry, thirsty, naked, and in need. He had to be buried in a borrowed tomb. 2 Cor. 9:8 promises us, an abundance for every good work."

6. Jesus bore our shame that we might share His glory.

7. Jesus endured rejection that we might have His acceptance as children of God. Jesus suffered rejection and shame for us.

"Jesus endured the cross, despising the shame." (Heb. 12:2) "For it was fitting for him, in bringing many sons to glory to make the captain of their salvation perfect through sufferings." (Heb. 2:10) Read Matt 27:46–50. Eph. 1:5–6 says He made us accepted in the beloved.

8. Jesus became a curse that we might receive a blessing. "Christ has redeemed us from the curse of the law...that the blessing of Abraham might come upon us." (Gal 3:13–14)

When Jesus had accomplished all this for us on the cross He said, "It is finished." The blessing of Abraham comes to us. "Bless" means to empower to prosper - spiritually, socially, physically and financially. We can be **immersed** in blessing. We can be immersed in peace.

These benefits come as a result of the work that Jesus did on the cross. They result from his obedience. All we need to do is trust and believe. There is, however, a greater degree of blessing than this.

The word "bless" in both the Hebrew and Greek languages has two levels to it. The first level could be called the "Barak" (Hebrew word) blessing. It is the blessing of covenant. The blessings of Abraham coming to us that believe, is an example. It is almost unconditional - except that we must believe. The second level is the Asher (Hebrew) blessing. It is a super blessing. It means you will be so blessed that you will be noticed and envied. It is conditional upon obedience. It is like having access to the tree of life. We must obey God's commands to get the Asher blessing.

The first level of blessing is accessed by faith. The work was done by Jesus, the blessing paid for by his effort. This corresponds to justification. Justification is by faith in the work of Jesus. His work saved you (and being saved is a great blessing). Justification is a process of salvation where you become teknon or a new born. A teknon is blessed at this level.

The second level of blessing - the super blessing - is also accessed by faith. The work is done by the Holy Spirit. The blessing is paid for by his effort. This corresponds to sanctification. God is at work in you and doing works through you. "For we are His workmanship, created in Christ Jesus for good works, which God prepared beforehand that we should walk in them." (Eph. 2:10) This refers to walking in the Spirit and to our goal of becoming huios. The second level of blessing requires the obedience of faith.

Chapter 14 introduced the two Greek words "teknon" and "huios". In case you don't remember, teknon is the legal offspring of the Father. It is what we become when we were adopted by God in a process called the new birth. Teknon has to do with the fact of birth or adoption. It has nothing to do with the maturity level of the child and stands in contrast to huios, which means mature. Huios means "one who matures and has the nature or character of the Father". Jesus said, "If you have seen me you have seen the Father". A huios of God exercises the power of God in the will of God. Our goal is to become exact duplicates of the Huios of God.

Becoming huios opens the way to the super blessing. The Greek word for "super blessed" is used in the Beatitudes. To obtain the super blessing one must obey God's instructions. God's instructions are given for the purpose of blessing us abundantly.

"Blessed are the poor in spirit, for theirs is the kingdom of heaven.
Blessed are those who mourn, for they shall be comforted.
Blessed are the meek, for they shall inherit the earth.

Blessed are those who hunger and thirst for righteousness, for they shall be filled.

Blessed are the merciful, for they shall obtain mercy.

Blessed are the pure in heart, for they shall see God.

Blessed are the peacemakers, for they shall be called sons (huios) of God.

Blessed are those who are persecuted for righteousness' sake, for theirs is the kingdom of heaven.

Blessed are you when they revile and persecute you, and say all kinds of evil against you falsely for my sake. Rejoice and be exceedingly glad, for great is your reward in heaven, for so they persecuted the prophets who were before you." Matt. 5:3–12

"I have come to give you life and that more abundantly." John 10:10

"Blessed are those who do His commandments, that they may have the right to the tree of life." Rev. 22:14

We were blessed by what Jesus did for us and we will have more blessing as we obey his commands.

A Musing 18: Exalted Happiness

"Blessed" (Greek - *makarioi*) in this next passage means "exceedingly happy". It is the Greek counterpart to *Asher* (Hebrew). It means to be so happy or joyful that others see the happiness and are envious of it. It is uncontainable happiness. Its bearer exudes happiness. *Barak* is the Hebrew word for bless that is often an unconditional promise from God. *Asher* is the promise of extra blessing that follows obedience to God's conditions.

Asher (makarioi) is not automatic, but the result of doing righteousness. The Greek word *makarioi* means "fully satisfied". It means the joy that comes from salvation not from the circumstances of life. Happy in English often is connected to luck or favourable circumstances. This "happy" is closer to joy in that regard. The blessedness outlined below is progressive and its progress depends on fulfilling the conditions Jesus sets down in these Beatitudes. (Matt. 5:1-12) "Beatitude" means exalted happiness.

"Exceedingly joyful are the poor in spirit, (the helpless – who realize their own spiritual helplessness – who see that that they can't make it happen; opposite of pride) for theirs is the kingdom (government) of God - the rule of the Spirit."

"Exceedingly joyful are those who mourn, (sorrow for their sins) for they shall be comforted." The Holy Spirit is the comforter.

"Exceedingly joyful are the meek, (meekness is strength under control. They see themselves as they truly are - servants) for they shall inherit the earth."

"Exceedingly joyful are those who hunger and thirst for righteousness, ("the hungering ones" hungering anew for another filling) for they shall be filled."

"Exceedingly joyful are the merciful, (caring attitude for those in misery, compassionate; outward focus) for they shall obtain mercy."

"Exceedingly joyful are the pure in heart, (subconscious, "pure" means 100%, continuous cleansing of the filter,) for they shall see God."

"Exceedingly joyful are the peacemakers, (knows the peace of God and brings it to others) for they shall be called sons (huios) of God."

"Exceedingly joyful are those who are persecuted for righteousness' sake, (highest level of exceedingly happiness) for theirs is the kingdom of God. Exceedingly joyful are you when they revile and persecute you, and say all kinds of evil against you falsely for my sake. Rejoice and be exceedingly glad, for great is your reward in heaven, for so they persecuted the prophets who were before you." Matt. 5:1–12

Chapter 20: Immersed in Joy

"That word you know, which was proclaimed throughout all Judea, and began from Galilee after the baptism which John preached: how God anointed Jesus of Nazareth with the Holy Spirit and with power, who went about doing good and healing all who were oppressed by the devil, for God was with Him." Acts 10:37–38

> "You have loved righteousness and hated lawlessness; Therefore God, your God, has anointed you with the oil of gladness more than your companions." Heb. 1:9

Jesus was immersed in water to fulfill all righteousness (Matt. 3:15). He was immersed in, or anointed with, the Spirit. Jesus was immersed in the joy of the Lord. As mentioned early in this book we are immersed in the love of God. That is a supernatural reality. We also can be immersed in joy. It is in fact God's will that we operate out of joy. In Kevin Dedmon's book *The Ultimate Treasure Hunt* he recommends we get filled up with the Spirit (until we are in effect drunk in the Spirit) before going out to do evangelism. He recommends we operate out of God's power and strength - his joy.

Jesus was anointed with the oil of gladness. It is unlikely you can get that particular fragrance at your local department store's cosmetic counter, but it is the fragrance Christians should be wearing. Ask God for more of his joy. Ask him to increase your capacity for joy. The kingdom of God is righteousness, peace and joy. If we are ruled by his government and obeying his instructions, then we should be immersed in joy. Obedience should bring joy.

"If you keep my commandments, you will abide in my love, just as I have kept my Father's commandments and abide in His love.

These things I have spoken to you, that my joy may remain in you, and that your joy may be full. This is my commandment, that you love one another as I have loved you." John 15:10–12

Legalism steals our joy. A wrong concept of grace, of it being an excuse to live in disobedience (license or lawlessness) also robs us of joy because we fail to attain the obedience of faith. Jesus loved righteousness and hated lawlessness and that resulted in an anointing of joy.

Two things are woefully missing in today's church:

1) A substantial tangible joy in the life of every believer.
2) A living association between righteousness (obedience) and joy.

Jesus wants his joy to remain in us and that our joy may be full. How do we allow his joy to remain? We pay attention to the things he has spoken to us. And what he has spoken is that we should keep his commandments the same way he kept his Father's commandments. How did he keep his Father's commandments? He only did what he saw his Father doing. He only said what he heard his Father saying. He walked in the Spirit.

Jesus is saying in John 15:10–12 that you'll have tremendous joy if you keep my commandments in the same way I kept my Father's commandments. In the great commission Jesus said, "Teach them to obey what I have commanded".

"Go therefore and make disciples of all the nations, baptizing them in the name of the Father and of the Son and of the Holy Spirit, teaching them to observe all things that I have commanded you; and lo, I am with you always, even to the end of the age." Matt. 28:19–20

Is it possible that part of the discipleship process included how to walk in joy? In the days of the early church did disciples learn how to obey the commands of Jesus in the way he modelled (hearing and obeying the Father)? If we obey his commands then our joy will be full. If you look at the great commission Jesus does mention his presence will be with them always. We know that in the presence of God is fullness of joy. So was Jesus thinking about the fullness of joy he promised in John 15 when he summarized his instructions in Matt.28:19–20?

I want his joy to remain. I want fulness of joy. Don't you? Look around at fellow believers, could they use a bit of that fulness as well? I'm not pointing the finger just to be critical of fellow believers. I'm just saying we could all use more joy. It's true isn't it? I don't just want the occasional laugh from hearing a good joke. I don't want any kind of substitute. I want the real deal and I want the full meal deal. It is apparent from context that the pathway to joy is to obey his commands, so I am prepared to believe God and obey. Even though some people might think I'm trying to earn salvation. Even though some people might think I'm legalistic. Even though there are people trying to obey God and it is joyless legalism, I'm determined to trust God that there is a way to obey using divine enablement (grace) that leads to joy.

Did you ever stop to think how much we miss because we weren't discipled? It's too bad the church discontinued discipleship. A system of academic lectures called sermons was substituted for the experience of apprenticeship by a real huios. Of course it is hard to find a huios these days. I am hoping that in the days ahead we will see them and they will disciple the next generation to be dynamic for God. I'm hoping to become one. I'm hoping you'll become one too.

So how do we keep the commandments of Jesus? What did Jesus share in John 15 that gives us insight into this? It is a worthwhile thing to find out, so we will start back in John 12 and I even suggest you read all of John chapters 12–15.

"For I have not spoken on my own authority; but the Father who sent me gave me a command, what I should say and what I should speak. And I know that His command is everlasting life. Therefore, whatever I speak, just as the Father has told me, so I speak." John 12:49–50

Jesus only did what he saw the Father doing (see John 5:19) and only spoke what he heard the Father speaking. (See John 12:49) Jesus knew the Word. He quoted scripture. He was well acquainted with the teachings of Moses and the words of the prophets. It seems that he was doing more than just following the written instructions of scripture. It seems he is interacting with God at a personal level. It seems that his obedience to God's commands was led of the Spirit. It was that personal interaction with God through the Spirit that brought life. Jesus says that he knows - he knows - that what God commands him is everlasting life.

The word of God is living and powerful. Hebrews 4:12 refers to the written word - the *logos* is living and powerful. The letter of the law kills but the Spirit gives life. Jesus was allowing the Spirit to make the Word alive. He wasn't following the letter of the law. "Not that we are sufficient of ourselves to think of anything as being from ourselves, but our sufficiency is from God, who also made us sufficient as ministers of the new covenant, not of the letter but of the Spirit; for the letter kills, but the Spirit gives life." (2 Cor. 3:5–6)

Paul wrote that our sufficiency is of God - that means he was not walking in his own strength or wisdom but by the grace of God. Paul had tapped into spiritual life that enabled him to minister in God's strength. It was the life that Jesus modelled. Read this next bit carefully.

"As the Father loved me, I also have loved you; abide in my love. If you keep my commandments, you will abide in my love, just as I have kept my Father's commandments and abide in His love. These things I have spoken to you, that my joy may remain in you, and that your joy may be full. This is my commandment, that you love one another as I have loved you. Greater love has no one than this, than to lay down one's life for his friends. You are my friends if you do whatever I command you." John 15:9–14

It all starts with abiding in his love. This book started with a look at the fact we are immersed in God's love. We are to abide in that love. How do we abide in his love? "If you keep my commandments, you will abide in my love." (John 15:10) How do we obey? We obey the same way Jesus obeyed the Father. How did Jesus obey the Father? He obeyed the Father by hearing and doing what the Spirit led him to do. Jesus was the Huios of God. A huios is led of the Spirit. (Rom. 8:14) He obeyed God by grace (God's indwelling enabling power). He used God's strength to obey God and so should we.

Jesus said, "You are my friends if you do whatever I command you to do". Are you prepared to do whatever he commands you to do? Do you want to be his friend? If so, then learn to abide in his love - learn to hear the Spirit and obey with his grace. **Become a huios**. Your joy will be full.

Chapter 21: Becoming Huios

"For the earnest expectation of the creation eagerly waits for the revealing of the sons of God." Rom. 8:19

We have touched on this theme already. Creation is waiting for the sons of God to be manifest. We aren't talking about a cult. We're talking about coming into sonship. We're talking about becoming like Jesus the Huios of God. We're talking about healing the sick and raising the dead, stopping storms and casting out demons. We're talking about taking on world religions like Islam and winning; of confronting the new age movement by being more spiritual than it is.

The bulk of the church today is comprised of teknons. Teknons are born-again Christians. They are converts. They have not matured spiritually yet. They haven't been discipled properly. They aren't doing much more than reading the Bible and attending meetings. According to one estimate I heard, 90% of Christians have never led another person to Christ outside of their own children. In places where the believers are going into the community and healing the sick, sinners are getting saved. Creation isn't eagerly waiting for teknons. It's waiting for saints that can "do the stuff."

By now you should be aware that there are two stages of growth. We become a teknon (a child) by the new birth and we become a huios (mature son) by being discipled in the Word and in the Spirit. Jesus said that to be great in God's kingdom you must become a servant. The Greek word is *"doulos"*. The writers of the Epistles called themselves doulos - bondservants. The kingdom of God is in the Holy Spirit and the kingdom is about serving Christ. You start in God's kingdom as a new born babe - his child - and as you grow up you follow the example of Jesus who took the form of a servant. You learn to serve using his strength - grace. Healing is a great example of this. You'll learn that though God told us to lay hands on the sick, we cannot heal them, but his grace can. As you learn to become led of the Spirit and begin to exercise faith over sickness and oppression, you become huios.

I trust that you want to become huios, or by now you would have lost interest in this book. There are several skills we can learn even though many of us do not have the tactical advantage of having a role model or disciple maker to follow (other than the Lord himself). We must spend time in his word and in his presence. We must learn to hear and obey the Holy Spirit. We must learn how to enter rest and operate out of divine power, not our own strength. We must risk doing what he says to do, trusting he will do it even when circumstances keep saying the opposite.

"...That the righteous requirement of the law might be fulfilled in us who do not walk according to the flesh but according to the Spirit." (Rom. 8:4) We must learn to walk according to the Spirit. We must become led of the Spirit. We must learn to hear and obey. The first skill to learn is to follow the leading of the Spirit. And chances are that you are going to have to forge ahead without a person handy to disciple you.

There are a few beliefs that will help to support you becoming Spirit-led. You will want to be convinced that God does love you - you are immersed in his love. He is committed to your success. It is also helpful to know that you are precious to God. Many of us suffer from feelings of not being good enough or having low self-images or feeling kind of useless. Maybe our fathers didn't value us or impart a sense of identity and destiny. To be brought up with those feelings conditions our heart (subconscious) to think we are not precious to God. Me telling you that you are indeed precious to God this one time may not undo 20 years of conditioning. You need to be healed on the inside, so take some steps to get healed.

Our church found 100 verses that affirm that God is for us and with us. They helped me to connect (at the subconscious level) with the truth that God really does love little ol' me. I, too, needed some inner healing to fully believe that I have value as a child of God before I even do any of his commands. We don't want to get into following his commands to earn or merit his love. We want to have a healthy understanding that by obeying his commands we simply go deeper into that existing love he already has for us. His commands will bring understanding and joy.

If you commit to becoming led of the Spirit, understand this, that God himself is more committed to it than you are. He has plans and methods to instruct you to become huios. Trust that it is his will. The best way to learn to know his voice is to read his Word over and over again. The Spirit is going to sound just like the Word, so learn the Word. Also it will help you if you have some people who are willing to take this journey with you. Others can provide encouragement and support. A log removed from the fire will soon cool and its flames go out.

Here are some practical things that you can do, to learn to hear the Spirit.

1. Ask God to fill you with the Spirit. (Daily)

2. Pray in the Spirit; sing in the Spirit. (Lots)

3. Ask God to tell you what he wants to speak about at the next church meeting. It might be an idea, a verse, or just a partial thought. Write it down. At the next meeting confirm if what you heard was accurate. If it was, then you know that both you and the speaker were on target.

4. Pray for God to help you become Spirit-led. You have not because you ask not. Make it a daily prayer. Actively seek to know his direction. Take time to practice.

5. Pray about where to direct your giving. The tithe belongs to the Lord so pay it to him personally. Then ask him where it is to go. Often he will direct it to something your church supports. We gave our members freedom to hear from God and direct the tithe to whatever he said, whether it was our church or not. Our church income increased. Pray about how much to give, and where. Don't just allow yourself to be manipulated by strong emotional appeal. You might be surprised, as you start to give where God directs you, how much positive feedback you will get.

6. Ask God to give you dreams in the night. This will help activate spiritual sensitivity. Then write down what you remember and research their meaning in the word of God.

7. Prophesy whenever possible. In our church we encourage prophetic prayer at every meeting. Then the prophecy is tested so the giver gets feedback if he has heard correctly or not. Feedback is easy to get. Simply ask the person you prophesied to, if it witnessed.

8. Try doing treasure hunting - as a group you have some safety. Read the book *The Ultimate Treasure Hunt* by Kevin Dedmon, if you have never heard of treasure hunting. You will be able to practice getting words of knowledge and healing the sick.

9. Spend as much time in his presence as you can. Some people "soak" by lying still and listening to worship music. This cultivates a greater awareness of his presence. Extended times of worship and praise help us grow.

10. Prepare teachings. Ask God to help you prepare teachings on different subjects. For example prepare a teaching on each physical method used in worship - bowing, clapping, shouting, singing, etc. and their spiritual significance. You learn more when you teach than you do when you're taught.

11. Obey hunches and later evaluate them. There is a risk. If you wait until you are 100% sure that you're hearing from God you will never act. Take a risk even if you are only 30% sure you are hearing from God. Do what you think he is saying and then the feedback will tell you if you were right.

12. Ask God for divine openings and divine appointments.

13. Listen to other people's testimonies and learn from their experience.

14. Persevere when you blow it. (You'll never develop skill without learning from mistakes).

15. Practice being thankful whenever God comes through for you - healings, divine insights divine appointments, hunches, dreams etc. - express enthusiastic gratitude.

16. Remember what you ask for. Remember what God directs. Keep a journal.

17. Avail yourself of excellent teaching by those that are being led of the Spirit. Listen to pod casts and DVDs. Read books. Attend conferences. Go on a mission trip like the one to Brazil with Randy Clark. Go to where God is moving and do what you can to learn from them.

18. Do whatever it takes because learning to be Spirit-led is vital.

Here in Canmore at the church I attend, we have restructured the way we do meetings. We no longer take up offerings. We encourage the saints to pray and hear for themselves. We no longer have sermons, we have discussions because we feel that everyone has something of value to contribute. We deliberately set things up to help the saints practice hearing from the Spirit.

We have prophetic prayer at every meeting. We allow anyone to share what they "see" during worship. We ask before the teaching times (dialogue style, not lecture style) if anyone heard what verse or theme God was going to speak about. We have set an agenda to provide a safe place to practice hearing and doing what the Spirit is saying. We believe that it is the job of five-fold ministers to equip the saints to do the work of the ministry. And what better way to equip them than to help them become Spirit-led?

Becoming Huios Review

The process of discipleship is all but lost to us and yet it is crucial to becoming huios. A person can only apprentice someone into something that they themselves walk in. I have some experience with apprenticing as I have apprenticed seven or eight into my trade. There was no classroom instruction. They had to work from day one and they learned on the job. We are a generation of believers that will have to disciple ourselves since no other options are available. Hopefully soon we can disciple others, and growing into huios will be accelerated.

I have noticed that there are two new catch words in our Christian vocabulary - activation and impartation. This is a definite step in the right direction, although it is just snippets of discipleship. Activation is where a teaching is given and then practised. Impartation is where an anointed person, lays hands on you to give you that same anointing. Impartation can propel one into a new and powerful ministry. We hear of people like Heidi Baker and Leif Hetlund, who had impartation from Randy Clark, so we know impartation really works. Here's the thing, Randy has laid hands on thousands of people but only a handful rise to world renown. What we don't know until we read their stories, is how prepared these two were to be launched. They were prepared by spiritual hunger, pain, heart break, experience, responsibility and "praying the price" to shoulder a greater anointing. In other words, they had been in a school of discipleship prior to the impartation.

Elisha had an impartation from Elijah. Joshua had one from Moses. They both had spent years being discipled first. The disciples had a mighty impartation on the day of Pentecost but it followed after three years of discipleship by the Huios. I seriously doubt that impartation will be a substitute for true discipleship. There are no short cuts for most of us. Paul took a short cut. He was blinded and knocked off his horse before his impartation. Then he spent 3 years in Arabia after his conversion and later 14 years in Syria and Cilicia (see Gal. 2:1) before he was given the right hand of fellowship by the elders in Jerusalem. (So maybe not a short cut after all)

My sense is that if the man of God has an oak tree anointing, what he will impart is an acorn. Take the acorn, plant and water it, and see what God will do. After all, it is God that does the imparting.

Chapter 22: Dimensions of Sonship

Sonship, or becoming huios, is a big topic, and different leaders in the body of Christ approach it from different angles. Some talk about having a relationship with the Father. They seem to skip over the discipleship message and go straight to having intimacy with the Father. In reality any kind of intimacy with the Lord involves obedience on our part. I listen to those who speak about intimacy with the Father. At first it seems they have discovered a subspace wormhole to sonship that bypasses serving and being discipled, but then as I hear more and more from them, I find elements in their own journey of obedience, submission, and serving. They may not articulate these elements clearly but they are there and they are important. Here are a few of the facets of sonship you may want to look into. Maybe my next book will develop this further.

1. Knowing the Father's Love

2. Entering into Our Inheritance & Knowing Our Destiny

3. Developing Relationship with the Father

4. The Power of Agape

5. Maturity - Spiritual, Emotional, and Social

6. Walking in the Spirit (Hearing and Obeying)

7. Confidence in Our Identity

8. Overcoming the Orphan Spirit

9. Functioning Out of Wholeness (physically and emotionally healed) No Love Deficit

10. Being Aligned with Heaven (Seeing God's Perspective)

11. On Assignment: Doing the Stuff, Healing the Sick, etc.

12. Secret Prayer Life of the Son

Maybe we should also add suffering to the list.

"When He had offered up prayers and supplications, with vehement cries and tears to Him who was able to save Him from death, and was heard because of His godly fear, though He was a Son, yet He learned obedience by the things which He suffered. And having been perfected, He became the author of eternal salvation to all who obey Him," Heb. 5:7–9

He learned obedience by the things which He suffered.

A Musing 19: Going on to Perfection

"For I will show him how many things he must suffer for my name's sake." Acts 9:16

One day a disciple in Damascus named Ananias was given a vision by God about a recent convert named Saul of Tarsus. Ananias was to heal Saul and give him a message. Part of the message was that Saul (Paul) was going to suffer many things. Talk about Good News! Ananias apparently didn't get the memo on properly sharing the gospel. He must have missed that seminar on how to win souls because you just don't tell people how much they must suffer. Heal them. Tell them God loves them. Tell them their sins are forgiven. Tell them God has a wonderful plan for their lives. But why bring up suffering?

Ananias didn't graduate from any of our schools of ministry. He simply allowed God to be Lord. He heard what the Spirit told him to say and do. And that's what he said and did. If you're going to follow a formula you might try the Ananias plan of following the leading of the Spirit. Apparently it works, since Paul didn't balk at the promise of God, that he would suffer, but fulfilled his calling. Although it might not have been one of the 4 points in the salvation plan you heard when you accepted the Lord, suffering may actually be part of God's wonderful plan.

"The Spirit Himself bears witness with our spirit that we are children of God, and if children, then heirs—heirs of God and joint heirs with Christ, if indeed we suffer with Him, that we may also be glorified together. For I consider that the sufferings of this present time are not worthy to be compared with the glory which shall be revealed in us." Rom. 8:16–18

Suffering is not popular but apparently it's in the small print.

"For to you it has been granted on behalf of Christ, not only to believe in Him, but also to suffer for His sake," Phil. 1:29

Paul was not dissuaded by the message Ananias gave, in fact, he later said "that I may know Him and the power of His resurrection, and the fellowship of His sufferings." (Phil. 3:10) Was Paul different from us? Was he deluded, or did he understand a portion of truth we have chosen for the most part to ignore? Is there something of value to be gained in suffering for Christ that can't be gained attending a seminar?

Paul seemed to have a positive attitude toward suffering - the reason for which may temporarily elude us. "I now rejoice in my sufferings for you, and fill up in my flesh what is lacking in the afflictions of Christ," (Col. 1:24) Suffering may be part of the process of attaining perfection.

"For it was fitting for Him, for whom are all things and by whom are all things, in bringing many sons to glory, to make the captain of their salvation perfect through sufferings." Heb. 2:10

"Though He was a Son, yet He learned obedience by the things which He suffered. And having been perfected, He became the author of eternal salvation to all who obey Him." Heb. 5:8–9

Suffering might be part of the plan for those of us who follow Jesus. "For to this you were called, because Christ also suffered for us, leaving us an example, that you should follow His steps:" 1 Peter 2:21

"Therefore, since Christ suffered for us in the flesh, arm yourselves also with the same mind, for he who has suffered in the flesh has ceased from sin," 1 Peter 4:1

And suffering might be a good thing. Joseph suffered in his journey to the throne. Jesus suffered in his journey to the throne. Is there a throne in your future?

Chapter 23: Obedience

> "Who being in the form of God, did not consider it robbery to be equal with God, but made Himself of no reputation, taking the form of a bondservant, and coming in the likeness of men. And being found in appearance as a man, He humbled Himself and became obedient to the point of death, even the death of the cross." Phil. 2:6–8

Jesus was a servant. He was obedient. He is the mold we are being poured into. He was a role model showing the way to live. Jesus, the Huios (Son) of God, was also called a servant of God. "The God of Abraham, Isaac, and Jacob, the God of our fathers, glorified His **Servant** Jesus, whom you delivered up and denied in the presence of Pilate, when he was determined to let Him go." (Acts 3:13)

"To you first, God, having raised up His Servant Jesus, sent Him to bless you, in turning away every one of you from your iniquities." Acts 3:26

"For truly against Your holy Servant Jesus, whom You anointed, both Herod and Pontius Pilate, with the Gentiles and the people of Israel, were gathered together to do whatever Your hand and Your purpose determined before to be done. Now, Lord, look on their threats, and grant to Your servants that with all boldness they may speak Your word, by stretching out Your hand to heal, and that signs and wonders may be done through the name of Your holy Servant Jesus." Acts 4:27–30

The scriptures speak to us of the expectation God has of our obedience to him.

Acts 6:7   "Then the word of God spread, and the number of the disciples multiplied greatly in Jerusalem, and a great many of the priests were obedient to the faith."

Acts 5:1   "Through Him we have received grace and apostleship for obedience to the faith among all nations for His name,"

Rom. 6:16   "Do you not know that to whom you present yourselves slaves to obey, you are that one's slaves whom you obey, whether of sin leading to death, or of **obedience** leading to righteousness?"

Rom. 15:17–19 "Therefore I have reason to glory in Christ Jesus in the things which pertain to God. For I will not dare to speak of any of those things which Christ has not accomplished through me, in word and deed, **to make the Gentiles obedient**— in mighty signs and wonders, by the power of the Spirit of God, so that from Jerusalem and round about to Illyricum I have fully preached the gospel of Christ."

2 Cor. 2:9 "For to this end I also wrote, that I might put you to the test, whether you are obedient in all things."

The Apostles saw themselves as servants. I am confident that they were also huios but they made it known that they were servants. It is a high calling.

Rom. 1:1   "Paul, a bondservant of Jesus Christ, called to be an apostle, separated to the gospel of God."

2 Cor. 4:5 "For we do not preach ourselves, but Christ Jesus the Lord, and ourselves your bondservants for Jesus' sake."

Phil. 1:1   "Paul and Timothy, bondservants of Jesus Christ, to all the saints in Christ Jesus who are in Philippi, with the bishops and deacons:"

James 1:1   "James, a bondservant of God and of the Lord Jesus Christ, to the twelve tribes which are scattered abroad: Greetings."

2 Pet. 1:1   "Simon Peter, a bondservant and apostle of Jesus Christ, to those who have obtained like precious faith with us by the righteousness of our God and Saviour Jesus Christ:"

Jude 1:1   "Jude, a bondservant of Jesus Christ, and brother of James, to those who are called, sanctified by God the Father, and preserved in Jesus Christ:"

Rev. 1:1   "The Revelation of Jesus Christ, which God gave Him to show His servants things which must shortly take place. And He sent and signified it by His angel to His servant John,

Our culture puts a high value on freedom so the bondservant message is not overly popular. We are, if we are honest, a bit suspicious of the whole obedience / bondservant issue. We do not want to be taken advantage of. Also we see being a servant in an unpleasant light. Bondservant sounds like bondage. And yet here we are, learning to be led of the Spirit so we can become huios, face to face with the undeniable reality that obedience is a topic addressed by the Word of God. We are called to be obedient and we are called to be bondservants.

My take on this, is that we have been lied to. We have been duped into thinking that being an obedient servant is a bad thing - something that is not fun at all. I have already alluded to the idea that obeying his commands brings Heaven to Earth - thy will be done on Earth as it is in Heaven. Maybe being an obedient servant is fun. Maybe it is life to us. Maybe we will like it. The adversary rebelled against God. He wanted to be independent and he perpetrates his message of independence from God to mankind. Let me ask you a question, who do you think has more fun - angels or demons? Who has a better life?

A Musing 20: Legalism

"You keep using that word. I do not think it means, what you think it means." - Inigo Montoya. *The Princess Bride*

Legalism may not mean what you think it means. Legalism is not the Law. Law means God's word or teaching. We are supposed to love the Law. (Rom. 7:22) God wrote the Law. The Law is good. Faith upholds it. Love fulfils it.

Rom. 3:10   "Love does no harm to a neighbour; therefore love is the fulfillment of the law."

Rom. 3:31   "Do we make void the law through faith? Certainly not! On the contrary we establish (uphold) the law."

Rom. 7:12   "Therefore the law is holy, and the commandments holy and just and good."

Rom. 7:14   "We know that the law is spiritual."

Rom. 8:6–7   "For to be carnally minded is death, but to be spiritually minded is life and peace. Because the carnal mind is enmity against God; for it is not subject to the law of God."

"Do not think that I came to destroy the Law or the Prophets. I did not come to destroy but to fulfill (make replete - fill to the brim). For assuredly, I say to you, till heaven and earth pass away, one jot or one tittle will by no means pass from the law till all is fulfilled (has come to pass). Whoever therefore breaks one of the least of these commandments, and teaches men so, shall be called least in the kingdom of heaven; but whoever does and teaches them, he shall be called great in the kingdom of heaven."
Matt. 5:17–19

Obedience to the Word in order to <u>merit</u> salvation is inappropriate but once you are saved by grace, obedience should be a way of life. Sadly for many Christians today the truth of obedience has been tainted by accusations that it's legalism.

Legalism can be described in at least four ways:

1. undue attention to rules and regulations,
2. others to conform to difficult standards without living it yourself or lifting a hand to help,
3. attempting to merit salvation by obeying the law (a common definition),
4. trying to live the Christian life in your own strength.

The Evangelical community has a strong focus on salvation - that we are justified by faith, not by works. This has led to the idea that any kind of work is an attempt to earn salvation. The Bible says we are created for good works. (Eph. 2:10) The works we are required to do after being saved are works of faith (obedience) that are done in His strength not our own. Grace saves us and works in and through us.

The only way we can obey is by grace. The life of grace is fuelled by prayer. The life of legalism is fuelled by pride. Legalism can be any attempt to obey without His grace or strength. It is evident when expectations of compliance are forced on people without consideration of God's patience, kindness, or High Priestly function of helping us overcome weaknesses.

And then I will declare to them, 'I never knew you; depart from me, you who practice lawlessness!'" (Matt. 7:23) In some circles, grace is taught as a substitute for law, the implication being that the law is obsolete now that grace has come. Jesus said that he did not come to abolish the law. (Matt. 5:17)

People that are disposed to hate the law or downplay its importance are **antinomian.** Antinomian means without law, or practising lawlessness. To the lawless, any genuine attempt on the part of a born-again Christian to walk in obedience of faith could potentially be misinterpreted as legalism. Paul wrote that with his mind he served the Law of God (Rom. 7:25). He wrote that the Law is spiritual (Rom. 7:14).

The new covenant makes the old covenant obsolete. (Heb. 8) The old way of doing things (the **system of law**) - sacrificing animals for your sins and obeying the commands in your own strength - is done away with. The new covenant includes God putting his Law in our minds and hearts and empowering us with His Spirit so we can obey the Law. His Law is **not** abolished, just the system of law is. The system of law is legalism. Legalism is any attempt to obey God in the power of human flesh, which, now that grace (divine power) has come, is obsolete.

"All Scripture is given by inspiration of God, and is profitable for doctrine, for reproof, for correction, for instruction in righteousness." 2 Tim. 3:16

If the law that God has written in our minds and heart is to work properly, it must be mixed with grace (the empowering presence of the Spirit). Law and grace must be mixed. That is how the new covenant works. The system of law (legalism) should not be (and cannot be) mixed with grace. Any attempts to merit God's salvation or his love, by human compliance to the law are futile. The system of the law is obsolete.

So to summarize:

1.   The law is good - very good.
2.   The system of the law (legalism) is bad - very bad.

Chapter 24: Lordship

I believe that God is love. I also believe that God is Lord. The Bible says twice that God is love and over 7000 times that he is Lord. Why is it that in 40 years of being a Christian I have heard 7000 messages on God's love and only two on his Lordship? Just lucky I guess. We need to be just as **immersed** in his Lordship as we are in his love.

The love message is crucial. It is foundational. We need to comprehend how precious we are to God and how committed he is towards us. We also need to relate to him as Lord. To relate to the Lord accurately requires that we see ourselves in the proper light. If he is your Lord then you are his servant. When we confess with our mouth that Jesus is Lord we aren't just assigning to him a title of honour. We are recognising that he is in charge. We commit to proceeding in life with the understanding that he is the master. We give up the throne and allow him to sit there.

And here is where our subconscious mind needs to be reconditioned. We have been brought up in a culture that perpetuates a false concept. We have been brought up to think that we are free, when in fact we are slaves to sin. Then we hear a gospel message that sounds as if we ask Jesus to be our Saviour, we can be free of sin's control and truly live free. Sin is taken off the throne and self can climb on. That is in fact an error. The Bible makes it crystal clear that we are to go from being a slave to sin to being a slave of righteousness. There are only two options - slave to righteousness or slave to sin. There isn't a third category - free to do whatever you like.

"Do you not know that to whom you present yourselves slaves to obey, you are that one's slaves whom you obey, whether of sin leading to death, or of obedience leading to righteousness? But God be thanked that though you were slaves of sin, yet you obeyed from the heart that form of doctrine to which you were delivered. And having been set free from sin, you became slaves of righteousness." Rom. 6:16–18

There is a malevolent force influencing us to think that there is a third category in between serving sin and serving God. Sort of like being a sinner saved by grace. We looked at that and there is no such thing. You are either a sinner or saved by grace. That 'third' category is, in actuality, simply slavery to sin. "Doing your own thing," means you are being controlled by sin. The only way to escape obeying sin is to obey God. And if obeying sin was fun at times (but later leads to death), could not obeying God be fun? Maybe it appears initially to be like death but leads to life. Bottom line - you only have two options. I think serving God is the better option.

Why is it we prefer to hear messages about love and not about Lordship? Have you ever heard that God's love in unconditional? What does that means exactly? It sounds like you don't have to do anything to get his love. We much prefer "unconditional" to serve and obey.

There is a truth buried in the concept of God's unconditional love. The problem with the concept is the packaging. So let's unpack it a bit. God loves sinners unconditionally. All they have to do - is be. God is adamant about the fact that he loves sinners. His love provided sinners with a way to escape sin and death. He stood at the door of a burning building and said, "Walk this way!" Some heeded his call and were saved and some did not and perished. Those that perished were loved no less than those who were saved. His love alone will not save you. You must obey him to be saved; obey in the sense of going with his plan of salvation.

You must confess with your mouth that Jesus is Lord in order to be saved. Therefore, although his love is unconditional, salvation is not. So the sinner that refuses to accept Jesus does not eternally benefit from God's love. He spends eternity in Hell. Hell is full of people God loves unconditionally.

God has an even greater love for those that he is in covenant with. Love is commitment. God is more committed to those who are in covenant with him. God loves all his children (by Adam) but he loves his bride more. The unconditional love message can miss the deeper love of covenant. "He who has my commandments and keeps them, it is he who loves me. And he who loves me will be loved by My Father, and I will love him and manifest myself to him." (John 14:21)

You might ask after reading this verse, "Didn't the Father already love them even before they loved back?" Yes he did. This refers to a greater revelation and experience of his love. The unconditional love message doesn't necessarily inspire us to press in. It could, but it can also inspire one to settle for less. The tree of life is available to those who obey, so don't settle.

The truth buried in the unconditional love concept is that his love is there even when we blow it. Nothing can separate us from his love. Nothing! God is for us and with us even when we disobey. That is not an excuse to disobey. As Paul says, "Is grace an excuse to sin? God forbid." It is not an excuse. It is a comfort. God never gives up on us. His unconditional love does **not** mean we are **not** called to obedience. It means he will help us to be obedient.

I think we do prefer to hear about his love more than hear about his lordship and I think leaders would rather preach love than lordship. Lordship has the unfortunate packaging of appearing to be legalism. If you are walking in lordship, then to those walking in license (lawlessness) you will appear to be in legalism. To those in legalism, lordship might appear to be license. Jesus walked in obedience to God (lordship) and yet to the Pharisees he was lawless. They didn't like him breaking their laws.

God said don't cook a kid (young goat) in its mother milk. "You shall not boil a young goat in its mother's milk." (Ex. 23:19, Ex.34:26, Deut. 14:21) The Orthodox Jews won't eat milk or milk products with meat. They even have two sets of dishes; - one for milk and one for meat. They even have two sets of sinks; - one for washing milk dishes and one for washing meat dishes. Maybe years ago a zealous Jewish leader thought, "If we aren't to cook meat in milk I'll go one better and not serve meat with milk". This restriction was an embellishment on God's instructions.

Jesus didn't line up with religious embellishment. He stuck to God's original intent. I have been a Christian for over 40 years and have had many cheese burgers and plenty of lasagna. During that time I never once cooked a young goat in its mother's milk. I have obeyed the Ex. 23:19 command as completely as the most kosher Rabbinical Jew.

Religion - not the good kind which is to visit widows, but the bad kind - is legalistic. The religious spirit tends towards making rules harder. The Bible teaches moderation. Don't get drunk. The religious spirit teaches abstinence. You can't have a glass of wine with supper. Never mind the fact that in Cana Jesus turned water into the equivalent of 738 bottles of wine. (Over 60 cases) That's a lot of Shiraz!

Where does it say in the Bible that you can't smoke? "Well brother, you are the temple of the Lord and you must not defile the temple." Funny, God filled Solomon's temple with smoke. Guess he missed that memo. "You can't sing in the choir if you smoke" was a rule in one church I attended. I have a better rule. You can't sing in the choir if you can't sing.

The Lord told his people not to carry their wares to market on the Sabbath. The Pharisees told them not to wear sandals that had nails in them on Saturdays because you mustn't lift metal on the Sabbath. The religious spirit gives obedience a bad name by complicating God's commands with a whole bunch of extra rules.

I began to keep the Sabbath about 20 years ago. I wouldn't work on Saturday's. I was a "tent builder" - someone who worked at a business as well as pastoring a church. I stopped working Saturdays. I still minister on Saturdays but I don't do business. I love the Sabbath. I look forward to it. Jesus said the Sabbath was made for man, not man for the Sabbath. The day of rest before Sunday gave me opportunity to wait on God and prepare for meeting on Sunday. I've had people tell me it's ridiculous to keep the Sabbath. Am I trying to earn my righteousness? I don't think so. I'm trying to please the Lord and enjoy all his benefits. Has it been a hardship to keep the Sabbath? Not for me. The benefits have far outweighed any minor inconveniences.

We have to see beyond the religious spirit and see the pure simplicity of obedience. In that pure simplicity is beauty and joy. Obeying Jesus will bring us into life. He loves us. Obeying legalism will bring us into death. We really need to be taught the commands of Christ in their pure form - without religious embellishment. Then maybe we can embrace obedience.

As I began to relate more and more to the Lordship of Jesus I often came face to face with my own failures. Lordship can bring a focus on obedience which in turn highlights any disobedience. Fortunately Jesus is more than Lord. I can relate to him as Saviour and as High Priest. Sometimes I have to spend time with the Saviour. Sometimes I go to my High Priest who understands my weaknesses. Sometimes I have to roll the responsibility of obedience onto my senior partner - the one I am yoked to. We are not called to obey in our own strength. We are called to obey in his power (grace). The joy of the Lord is my strength. I think we can enjoy being immersed in his lordship.

A Musing 21: Hearing

> "My sheep hear my voice, and I know them, and
> they follow me." John 10:27

Years ago I had the joy of going salmon fishing at a proper fishing camp on the coast of British Columbia. Unfortunately, being inexperienced, I didn't catch any fish. It was frustrating. Then a friend told me how to set the tension on my line properly and I began catching fish. A simple "tweaking" of the tension meant the difference between success and failure.

Are you hearing from God clearly? A small tweaking might make you more successful. Most Christians hear the voice of God to a degree. Many of the Old Testament references to obeying the voice of God actually mean obeying the word God gave Moses - so not a literal hearing of a voice but rather adhering to what God has said in the past. If we truly want to hear the voice of God we start by reading and obeying the written Word. So if you are doing that, then you are already hearing his voice to a point. You can also hear him in real time.

Jesus said that his sheep can hear his voice. When they do, they follow. If you want to hear God speak to you, be prepared to obey what he says, no matter how foolish it many seem. We were in the Ukraine teaching at the Ternopil YWAM base. My friend heard from God to give flowers to the DTS leader. It seemed foolish to him, but it meant a great deal to her. If you are afraid to do "foolish" things then fear will prevent you from hearing God clearly.

Part of developing a hearing ear is to get to know the Lord by spending time with him. Generally speaking, it is easier to hear from God if we are in prayer and worship and reading the Word in our personal quiet times. Knowing the Word will help us discern the voice of God. Praying in the Spirit or in tongues also helps a great deal. Jude 20 gives valid advice. "But you, beloved, build yourselves up on your most holy faith, praying in the Holy Spirit."

It is easier to hear if we listen. Sometimes ideas pop into mind that we dismiss. Sometimes the voice we hear is just our own inward voice. One fisherman to another - and here comes the tweaking - God's voice will sound like your inward voice. You are hearing from God! Now test it. Compare it to the written Word and if it passes, do it.

Chapter 25: The Commands of Christ

Jesus said, "Make disciples, teaching them to obey all that I have commanded you." (Matt 28:19–20) If I were to ask a Christian to list all of the commands of Jesus he would know them by heart, right? Can you list them all? Why do Christians who are supposed to be disciples of the Lord not know the commands of Christ? It's sort of like the Christians who are king dumb.

Let's put this into perspective. Jesus is Lord. He did tell his disciples to make new disciples by teaching them to obey all that he commanded. That process of reproduction was disrupted even before the end of the first century. We haven't quite recovered from that, but God is restoring his truth to the Church. Jesus set up his kingdom with two components - his disciples and his Spirit. All that we do in the kingdom is done by the power of the Spirit.

One of the important commands Jesus gave was to heal the sick. If you have tried to heal the sick, you might have noticed it is hard to do without him doing it. Some other commands include open blind eyes, cast out demons and raise the dead. It is somewhat obvious that these commands require supernatural power - so we have to trust God to help. Why not trust God to help with all his commands?

In the new covenant God has provided his Spirit. "I will put my Spirit within you and cause you to walk in my statutes, and you will keep my judgments and do them." (Ezek. 36:27) The Spirit enables us to obey God. So we need to learn to obey all his commands using the strength of the Spirit. We aren't to do it in our own strength.

To me his first command is Deut. 6:4–9. It's not really technically the first, but it is a prominent one. Jesus said it was the greatest.

"Hear, O Israel: The Lord our God, the Lord is one! You shall love the Lord your God with all your heart, with all your soul, and with all your strength. And these words which I command you today shall be in your heart. You shall teach them diligently to your children, and shall talk of them when you sit in your house, when you walk by the way, when you lie down, and when you rise up. You shall bind them as a sign on your hand, and they shall be as frontlets between your eyes. You shall write them on the doorposts of your house and on your gates." Deut. 6:4–9

The first command was **"hear"**. It is the same today. The first thing is to hear what the Spirit is saying. Hear and then obey. You can ask for help in between. You hear, you say "God help me," and you do. Notice that in Deuteronomy the words (of his commands) were to be in their hearts. That sounds just like the new covenant in Heb. 8:10. The heart is the subconscious mind. It is programmed by repetition. Notice that God tells his people to repeat his commands and to disciple their children by teaching them to obey all that he commanded. They were to **immerse** themselves in his Word.

Hebrews picks up on that thought and says, "Today if you will hear his voice; do not harden your hearts." Hearing is vital, and the heart is not to be hardened but reprogrammed with the Word so as to be ready to comply with the instructions you are hearing. The children of Israel disobeyed God the first time he sent them into battle and then they later decided to fight without God's help. That was pride.

Pride hardens the heart. Pride says, "I can do this myself!" The measure of pride in a man is equal to the inverse of how much he prays. If one has much pride he prays little. We need to be constantly praying in the Spirit.

Pride makes us think that we can obey the commands of Jesus in our own strength or that God will not help us. It's silly really. God knows we need his help and is willing to provide it. Keep the ears open. Ask God to help you hear. Hear God's heart!

"Oh, that they had such a heart in them that they would fear me and always keep all my commandments, <u>that it might be well with them</u> and with their children forever! Go and say to them, 'Return to your tents.' But as for you, stand here by me, and I will speak to you all the commandments, the statutes, and the judgments which you shall teach them, that they may observe them in the land which I am giving them to possess. 'Therefore you shall be careful to do as the Lord your God has commanded you; you shall not turn aside to the right hand or to the left. You shall walk in all the ways which the Lord your God has commanded you, <u>that you may live and that it may be well with you</u>, and that you may prolong your days in the land which you shall possess.'" Deut. 5:29–33

God has expectations:

1. God expects us to obey his commands.

2. God expects us to use his power (grace) to obey (not to be proud and try to obey in human strength).

3. God expects us to teach his commands using repetition (and model by doing it).

4. God expects us to hear Him direct us to a particular command.

5. God expects that obedience will benefit us.

Jesus said, "I only do the things the Father tells me to do or say the things the Father tells me to say." Jesus modelled hearing and he modelled doing - by using grace, the power of the Spirit - to do it. That is what we are to do. We program our heart with the Word. We hear what the Spirit is directing us to do at that moment and we ask God for help to do it and step out in faith. Lay hands on the sick and they will recover.

I lay hands on and the Spirit heals. We move forward by trusting him. It's God's job to put his Spirit into you. It's your parent's job (or the one discipling you, or your job) to put the commands into you. We do what we can do and God does the rest.

Just to help you, I have provided a short list of Christ's commands. As you read them you will probably find you already know them. Try to reflect on them in terms of partnering with the Lord to obey them. Let his Spirit - his grace - do the work.

The Commands of Christ

To see and enter his kingdom:
- Repent (change your perspective of who Jesus is: turn from sin)
- Believe in Jesus as Lord
- Be water baptized (immersed)
- Be filled with the Spirit (baptism)

Ongoing practice:
- Repent (conform your thinking to God's perspective)
- Believe (trust the Lord)
- Be (being) filled with the Spirit
- Love God & abide in God's love (express love for the Lord in praise & worship and express love for the Lord by obedience to his word)
- Ten Commandments with the Jesus upgrades
- Seek first the government of God (seek to be led of the Spirit; serve God) Matt. 6:33

- Walk in the Spirit (see what God is doing & saying and do & say that)
- Be yoked to Jesus, enter rest, and operate out of joy
- Heal the sick, open blind eyes, open deaf ears
- Raise the dead, cast out demons
- Preach the kingdom
- Humble yourself; resist the devil
- Tithe to God personally
- Give generously
- Forgive constantly
- Pray without ceasing
- Fast
- Love one another as he loves us (There are about forty "one another's")
- Serve people in the love and power of God
- Do and teach (role model) the Word
- Go and make disciples

Chapter 26: Entering into Rest

The Lord spent forty years teaching the children of Israel to rest on the Sabbath. He called it humbling them. "And you shall remember that the Lord your God led you all the way these forty years in the wilderness, to **humble** you and test you, to know what was in your heart, whether you would keep His commandments or not." (Deut. 8:2)

Let us enter the rest God has for us. (Hebrews 4) It does require faith and humility. "Therefore, since a promise remains of entering His rest, let us fear lest any of you seem to have come short of it." Heb. 4:1

"For we who have believed do enter that rest, as He has said:"Heb.4:3 "Since therefore it remains that some must enter it, and those to whom it was first preached did not enter because of disobedience, again He designates a certain day, saying in David, 'Today,' after such a long time, as it has been said: 'Today, if you will hear His voice, Do not harden your hearts.'" Heb. 4:6–7

"For if Joshua had given them rest, then He would not afterward have spoken of another day. There remains therefore a rest for the people of God. For he who has entered His rest has himself also ceased from his works as God did from His. Let us therefore be diligent to enter that rest, lest anyone fall according to the same example of disobedience." Heb. 4:8–11

We enter into rest when we cease from our own labours and believe God to do it. We enter into rest when we learn to do the things we are called to do, using grace, not human effort. We enter into rest when we learn to walk in the Spirit.

In Exodus the 31st chapter, there is the story of God anointing a craftsman to help build his Tabernacle. The building took place because the Spirit was in place. Immediately after the mention of the craftsman anointing, God spoke about the Sabbath. I think the two thoughts are connected. I think God is saying work with the anointing. He is saying stop working with human strength and come into his rest. Operate out of humility, not pride. Use divine strength, not human strength. Burn the oil, not the wick! "Come to me, all you who labour and are heavy laden, and I will give you rest." (Matt. 11:28)

Let Jesus do the work - at least all the heavy lifting.

I Have Entered His Rest

Hebrews 4 tells us that the promise of entering his rest still remains. Have you entered his rest? The steps one must take to enter the rest God promises are simple. Hebrews 4:1-16 explains them. It is briefly summarized below.

A promise remains.
The **gospel** was preached.
We who **believe** do enter that rest.
Those that were disobedient did not enter.
He who has entered God's rest has ceased from his own **works** (human effort).
Let us be **diligent** to enter that rest.
We have a great High Priest who knows our weaknesses.
Let us come boldly to the throne of grace to obtain mercy and grace.

You enter the rest of God when you believe the gospel. Believing in this context carries the component of obedience. We understand that it is not our works - doing the system of the law with human effort - that saves us, but trusting in the finished works of Jesus. We cease from trying to please God, to earn his love, or to attain righteousness through human effort. When we simply, by the obedience of faith, accept that God already loves us and has provided salvation for us by giving us his righteousness in Christ, then we enter His rest. We must be diligent not to slip back into the system based on human effort (legalism) but to stay in grace. We are going to blow it at times but we have a High Priest who is aware of our every weakness and has covered every contingency. We can come boldly into the throne room, based on the merits of Jesus, and obtain mercy and grace.

The gospel is the good news that God himself has made a way of salvation. The Jews had taken the law of God and changed it. They modified it into a way to attain righteousness. They thought if they obeyed all 613 commands it would make them worthy. They turned the law into a system for attaining favour without realizing that they already had access to God's favour. Favour is grace. Grace is divine empowerment. Grace is the opposite of human effort. It is divine effort. The law of God is the teaching of God. The system of the law is an attempt to obey God's teaching in human strength. When we cease from these human works we enter His rest.

Galatians tells us we must be diligent. Having begun in faith and grace, let us not embellish God's plan with adjuncts and addendums that bring us back into serving God in human effort. We must continue in the walk that began with trusting in Christ for salvation by learning to operate in grace. We attained righteousness when we repented and believed the gospel. Jesus took our sin and gave us his righteousness. Sometimes our own weakness confronts us, which can result in self-condemnation. God has an answer. He is our High Priest. He intercedes for us. Then when we realize God loves us even in our weakness, we can come with boldness to the throne of Grace to get mercy and grace. Our prayers for divine help are answered and we are at rest operating out of grace, not works.

Have you taken the necessary steps? It occurs to me at this point that some readers may not know what steps to take exactly. If you have gone to church but never confessed with your mouth that Jesus is Lord, then you might want to know how to do it. If you are a spiritual person but have never really had a definitive experience with the Holy Spirit, then you too may want to know how to connect with God in a simple biblical way.

First you must repent. Chances are you have already repented. By the time you have read this far, in this book, you most likely believe that Jesus is more than a swear word. Have you confessed that he is Lord of your life? You might pray, "God, I believe that Jesus is in fact Lord." You might be like I was. I started with a very simple confession. I said, "God if you are real and Jesus is who these people (the church where I heard the gospel) say he is, then I want to know. If you can show me then I will follow you."

For the next two steps, you might need to find some Spirit-filled Christians who will assist you. You can wait until they can pray for you to receive the Holy Spirit or you can ask the Father to fill you with the Holy Spirit right now. Some people have been filled privately, but most are baptized in the Holy Spirit when others prayed for them. To be baptized in water requires that others are involved. You will also need access to a pond or pool or river. Water baptism, you will remember, cuts you off from the old support system. It cuts you off from sin's control. Spirit baptism connects you with a new support system and empowers you to obey God.

Taking these simple steps insures that you see and enter the kingdom of God. You are a teknon. You have come under new management. You are immersed in his covenant love. Read his Word. Learn to hear and obey his Spirit. Learn to serve using grace. Take the steps toward becoming huios. Ask God for joy.

A Musing 22: Brazil was a Thrill

My experience in Brazil with Global Awakening was excellent. My wife and I went there to be part of the prayer team. Most of those of the 80 that went, want to go back. When you go on a trip with Global Awakening, they connect you with the other team members on Facebook. Every day I get comments from team members, of the change in their life that being in Brazil has brought.

While we were in Brazil we attended evening meetings at various churches in Sao Paulo. The speakers were members of Global Awakenings staff. Those on the prayer team were to call out a word of knowledge and later pray for the sick. It was remarkably easy. The first night I prayed with two individuals to be baptized in the Spirit. They were. All around were people praying and getting prayed for. In the course of the trip there were 1653 recorded healings. There were 241 first time decisions for Christ.

The first word of knowledge I gave in San Paulo, was that someone had a sore right elbow. OK, so it wasn't a huge dynamic word, but it was what I got, so I gave it. It was a little scary. What if I heard wrong? Not that anyone in that crowd would remember my word or what I look like, but I was a bit self-conscious. The last person to testify that night to a healing said that their right elbow was healed. Thank-you Jesus! In Brazil we took some small risks. We stepped out of our comfort zones and saw God move.

All I did was lay my hands on people and pray and they were healed. It was amazing. It took very little effort on my part - just the energy to extend a hand and say a few words. God did the work. It was fun. It was fun seeing God heal people. Serving God can be fun. If only we could apply that to every aspect of our walk with the Lord. I think that letting Jesus be Lord of our whole life could be as fun as healing in Brazil was. Like scuba diving is fun once you overcome the fear of the water. Some saints fear total surrender to the Lord. I'm saying take the plunge! Become totally immersed in God.

Going to Brazil wasn't all fun. In fact I was going to call this musing – "Brazil was a thrill but now I need a sleeping pill." We had to fly on a red eye to Brazil, we were up late most nights, and the climate is hotter than this Canadian prefers - so I accumulated a bit of a sleep deficit on the trip. I even commented to Pat Bock, the international director of Global Awakening, that perhaps "Awakening" should be changed to "Sleep Deprivation" to more accurately reflect what happens on their mission trips. The point is - it was worth it. It was fun being used of God. And even though I was sleep deprived most of the time, when we were ministering I was never tired. The grace of God was there.

John Wimber has shared that when he first started teaching on healing, they went two years without anyone getting healed. Someone asked him what he learned in those two years. John replied, "I learned I can't heal anyone." Then healing broke out and soon people were getting healed and blind eyes were opening. What did John learn then? He learned that God can heal.

We need to understand that the life is in the Spirit. God can live the Christian life even if we cannot. We need to enter into rest and let Jesus take over. That's what grace is all about. Grace is when God does the work. All we have to do is humble ourselves and let him. Learning to hear is the key. Learning to hear - waiting for him to direct - is the key to operating in grace. We are like little children or puppy dogs that like to run ahead. Walk with the master, not ahead of him. Listen and do.

We cannot heal cancer, but God can. We cannot easily overcome bitterness, but God can. We cannot love the unlovely, but God can. We can't forgive 70 times 7, but God can. We can't even remember to read our Bible every day, but God can. We need to trust in his ability, not our own. This is why learning to be led of the Spirit is so vital. It is the way to living on his terms with his power.

"For as many as are led by the Spirit of God, these are the sons of God." Rom. 8:14

Chapter 27: Totally Immersed

"For we know how dearly God loves us, because he has given us the Holy Spirit to fill our hearts with his love." Rom. 5:5 NLT

I want all that God has for me. I am greedy for more of Him. Like the old hymn says, I want the things of earth to grow strangely dim in the light of his glory and grace. Leif Hetlund was baptized in the love of God. It radically changed his life, his marriage, his family, and his ministry. Somehow God was able to impart to Leif a comprehension - an understanding - an experience of his love. Leif is **immersed** in the 4 dimensional love of God.

"That you, being rooted and grounded in love, may be able to comprehend with all the saints what is the width and length and depth and height to know the love of Christ which passes knowledge; that you may be filled with all the fullness of God." Eph. 3:18–19

I have talked to Leif and I do not understand God's love nearly as well as he does. It is one of those things better felt than "telt". But I do understand enough to be hungry for more of his love. Knowing God's love for us is extremely valuable. I shared how we as a church looked up a hundred verses in the Bible that express that God is for us and with us - that he loves us deeply. It is important to allow the Word to dwell in us richly - especially to allow it to reprogram our subconscious (heart) to make it a proper filter. We need to "get" the message of Eph. 3:18–19.

"Now hope does not disappoint, because the love of God has been poured out in our hearts by the Holy Spirit who was given to us." Rom. 5:5

"In Him you also trusted, after you heard the word of truth, the gospel of your salvation; in whom also, having believed, you were **sealed** with the Holy Spirit of promise, who is the guarantee of our inheritance until the redemption of the purchased possession, to the praise of His glory." Eph. 1:13–14

The kingdom of God is the government of God or the rule of Christ (in us). It is being governed or led of the Spirit. We are to make seeking this our first priority. The government of God is described in Romans 14:17 as righteousness, peace and joy.

Righteousness in this passage has to do with right doing or right living. It has to do with doing the will of God. "I will be your God." It is about lordship. Do you also remember that love is a commitment to do what is right regardless of emotion? When God imparts love - the love of God has been poured out in our hearts - he imparts a desire to walk in his will. And by so doing he carves out in us a greater capacity for more of his peace and joy.

We were made righteous before God by the gift Jesus gave us that he paid for - righteousness. This is righteousness of right standing or right being. This was given to us when we confessed with our mouth and believed in our heart that Jesus is indeed Lord and master. To this gift, God adds grace, in order that we may rule in life over darkness, sickness, and poverty. That grace is the Holy Spirit. The Holy Spirit helps us take the next step of right doing. We need the Spirit each step of the way and as we learn to hear and trust in Him we become led of the Spirit - we walk in the Spirit. Then we have become huios.

Kingdom righteousness means we obey the Lord in the power of the Spirit. We cannot obey properly in our own strength. Serving God in human strength equals burn out.

I was teaching at a seminary in Yalta. Yalta is on the Black Sea and the folks there commonly see people waterskiing. My message was being translated into Russian by Sophia my interrupter (interpreter). One evening in class, I said, "Trying to live the Christian life without the Holy Spirit is like trying to waterski behind a row boat." I thought that I had given a brilliant word picture. It was both wise and amusing. No one in the class got it. They all looked blank. I looked at Sophia and asked her what she had said. She told me. "Trying to live the Christian life without the Spirit is like trying to water ski behind a robot." It can be difficult trying to paint a word picture in Russian. I hope you got the message that you can't do it in your own strength.

Righteousness relates to lordship. It is the part of being led of the Spirit where we submit to doing what we have heard from God to do. It leads to peace and joy. It is almost like righteousness is a container for peace and joy. We want the container's capacity to increase. Obeying God is something to be desired. We need to be immersed in his kingdom - in his lordship. Being immersed in his lordship is walking in the Spirit.

The kingdom is in the Holy Spirit and we are to be immersed in the Spirit. Let the Spirit be poured out more and more. Come Holy Spirit and fill us. To be filled is vital. It is a step towards being led and empowered by the Spirit as in Luke 4:1–13. "Then Jesus, being filled with the Holy Spirit, returned from the Jordan and was led by the Spirit into the wilderness." (Luke 4:1) There Jesus fasted and was tempted. "Then Jesus returned in the power of the Spirit to Galilee, and news of Him went out through all the surrounding region." (Luke 4:13) God is not just looking for Spirit-filled teknons but for Spirit-led and Spirit-empowered huios. First we must be immersed (filled) with the Spirit, but then we go forward and deeper.

When we are filled with his government, that government can spill over into people's lives. His government is one of peace. His government of peace spills out in the form of healing, health, deliverance, sight for the blind, prisoners set free, prosperity and provision, strength, confidence, and rest. As his people we can access all heaven has.

His government has an inward component - we obey the Lord and do what is authorized. It has an outward component - we heal the sick and preach the gospel with signs following. Both components should delight us.

His government is joy. It is the joy of his presence. "I am with you always." We are to get into his presence, soak in his presence, align with his thoughts in his presence, be fully saturated and totally immersed in his presence, and then leak his presence everywhere we go. His joy is our strength.

Joy can also mean grace. Grace is God's power and joy is God's strength. We are to live using God's strength - his power. How do we get his strength and power? We get his joy and grace by asking for it. Grace is accessed by humility - he gives grace to the humble, and by faith. The word "humble" means "being real". John Wimber was being real when he said he couldn't heal anyone. We ask and we wait for God's timing. Waiting can be the hard part. We need to be patient - wait for it, like Mary in John 20.

"Now on the first day of the week Mary Magdalene went to the tomb early, while it was still dark, and saw that the stone had been taken away from the tomb. Then she ran and came to Simon Peter, and to the other disciple, whom Jesus loved, and said to them, "They have taken away the Lord out of the tomb, and we do not know where they have laid Him.""

"Peter therefore went out, and the other disciple, and were going to the tomb. So they both ran together, and the other disciple outran Peter and came to the tomb first. And he, stooping down and looking in, saw the linen cloths lying there; yet he did not go in. Then Simon Peter came, following him, and went into the tomb; and he saw the linen cloths lying there, and the handkerchief that had been around His head, not lying with the linen cloths, but folded together in a place by itself. Then the other disciple, who came to the tomb first, went in also; and he saw and believed. For as yet they did not know the Scripture, that He must rise again from the dead. Then the disciples went away again to their own homes."

"But Mary stood outside by the tomb weeping, and as she wept she stooped down and looked into the tomb. And she saw two angels in white sitting, one at the head and the other at the feet, where the body of Jesus had lain. Then they said to her, "Woman, why are you weeping?" She said to them, "Because they have taken away my Lord, and I do not know where they have laid Him.""

"Now when she had said this, she turned around and saw Jesus standing there, and did not know that it was Jesus. Jesus said to her, "Woman, why are you weeping? Whom are you seeking?" She, supposing Him to be the gardener, said to Him, "Sir, if you have carried Him away, tell me where you have laid Him, and I will take Him away." Jesus said to her, "Mary!" She turned and said to Him, "Rabboni!" (Which is to say, Teacher)." John 20:1–16

Mary came early and lingered on after Peter and John had left, and she saw Jesus. Let's linger in the presence and learn to feel the presence, and from that, learn to operate out of rest. Burn the oil, not the wick. We can enter his presence in worship. Enter his gates with gratitude. Enter his courts with praise (teHillah - new songs, singing in the Spirit). Enter his presence, stay in his presence, and soak in his presence. And pray, asking him to fill, lead, and empower you with his Spirit.

Jesus entrusted part of the responsibility for spreading the message of the kingdom to his disciples. They were to wait until they received power in the form of the indwelling Holy Spirit. Their part was to walk in the Spirit and to obey and to teach His commands. They were to make disciples. The importance of making disciples was lost to us. Now we find ourselves seeing the possibility of becoming *huios* without an older *huios* around to disciple us into it. This is an obstacle to our spiritual growth, but one that God will help us overcome.

We can read books, attend seminars, and fellowship with like-minded saints. We can do treasure hunts, ask for divine appointments, and use the gifts of the Spirit in the marketplace. We can read and study the Word, and allow it to reprogram our subconscious. We can ask the Father to help us to be led of the Spirit - to become huios. Then we can disciple others.

I think that what the world and the church need to see is Christians who are truly immersed in the Lordship of Christ and who are lovin' it. It's not legalism. It's not license. It's true obedience that is life giving and full of joy. It's about saints that have yielded to the master and are filled with his love and power. They are doing the stuff. They are operating out of rest. They are full of grace. The world and the church - the whole of creation - needs to see the revealing - the glory - of the Spirit-led and empowered ones - the huios of God. Are you going to be one of them? Yes. Of course, yes.

> "For I consider that the sufferings of this present time are not worthy to be compared with the glory which shall be revealed in us. For the earnest expectation of the creation eagerly waits for the revealing of the sons of God." Rom. 8:18–19

Glossary of Terms

Agape	commitment to do right regardless of emotion
Antinomian	without or against the law, practising lawlessness
Baptize	to dip or immerse
Born Again	to come under new management
Doulos	slave or bondservant; has surrendered his will to the master
Grace	divine power, divine strength, or divine effort; the empowering presence of the indwelling Holy Spirit.
Heart	subconscious mind - filter; source of speech, organ of thought, treasury of memories; seat of true faith
Huios	Greek word for mature son: a follower of Christ who is Spirit-led. Not gender specific. One who reveals the nature of the Father.
Joy	gladness; grace or favour; the presence of God; divine strength
Kingdom	form of government, monarchy; 'mono' meaning one, 'archy' meaning rule
Kingdom of God	government of God; rule of Christ (Spirit - Christ in you); lordship of Jesus

Legalism	an attempt to obey God by human effort; the system of the law; prideful attempt to merit salvation or God's love or righteousness through works or human effort.
Peace	the benefits - of the cross, of access to Heaven's resources, of divine government.
Replete	to fill fuller; to top up; to make full
Righteousness	1) the gift of "right standing" paid for by Jesus on the cross; 2) the fruit of "doing right" which is serving Christ - doing his will in the power of the Spirit.
Teknon	Greek word for legal offspring - by birth or adoption. Seed of the Father.
Yoke	instrument designed to extract work from an animal; easy means padded

Books by the same author available at Amazon.com

Understanding the Kingdom of God (2009 Xlibris Corp) 75 pages

Short read designed for new or established believers that can be used for group study. It focusses on the new birth from a kingdom perspective. It defines the kingdom and the gospel of the kingdom. Even non-Christians have read it and benefited.

Kingdom Foundations for Supernatural Living (2012 Destiny Image Europe) 173 pages

An expanded version of *Understanding the Kingdom of God* which includes a detailed look at heart faith, serving as a doulos and becoming a huios. Also includes a template for house groups to help create an atmosphere where people can learn to be led of the Spirit.

Ian Wilkinson first met the Lord in 1971 during the Jesus People Movement. He has a Bachelor of Science and a Bachelor of Education from the University of Calgary. Ian taught Junior High School science. He has operated his own business for many years. He pastored in Canmore for ten years at the New Life Centre and more recently pioneered the vision for Huios House. He has led Huios House for over five years and overseen the transformation of the New Life Centre from a typical pastor-led church into a new wine skin that promotes body ministry and becoming huios, and is overseen by a plurality of functioning elders. He has travelled much, teaching on the kingdom in churches, pastor's seminars, home groups and seminaries in the UK, the Ukraine, the Philippines, Malawi Africa, the US and Canada.

He lives with his wife Melodie in Canmore, Alberta. They have three grown children and four grand-children. All three children are certified scuba divers. Melodie may yet one day take the plunge. Maybe the grandchildren will beat her to it.

Contact information:

Ian Wilkinson
New Life Centre
28 216 Three Sisters Drive
Canmore, AB Canada T1W 2M2

Website: www.nlccanmore.com
The website has email information.